Parke Flourney

The search lights of St. Hippolytus

Parke Flourney

The search lights of St. Hippolytus

ISBN/EAN: 9783337270179

Printed in Europe, USA, Canada, Australia, Japan

Cover: Foto ©Andreas Hilbeck / pixelio.de

More available books at **www.hansebooks.com**

THE SEARCH-LIGHT OF ST. HIPPOLYTUS

THE PAPACY AND THE NEW TESTAMENT IN THE LIGHT OF DISCOVERY

BY

PARKE P. FLOURNOY

WITH AN INTRODUCTION BY

PROF. WALTER W. MOORE, D.D., LL.D.

OF UNION THEOLOGICAL SEMINARY, VIRGINIA

NEW YORK   CHICAGO   TORONTO

FLEMING H. REVELL COMPANY

1896

THE NEW YORK TYPE-SETTING COMPANY
THE CAXTON PRESS

TO THAT GREAT AND GOOD TEACHER OF MANY
GRATEFUL PUPILS, THE
REV. R. L. DABNEY, D.D., LL.D.,
ONE OF THEM AFFECTIONATELY DEDICATES
THIS VOLUME

CONTENTS

INTRODUCTION

A SHORT and readable book dealing in a popular way with certain claims of the Romish Church, and certain theories of modern rationalism in regard to the authority of Scripture, on the one hand, and the genuineness of certain portions of Scripture, on the other, is a desideratum of our contemporary Christian literature. The demand for such a work is emphasized by the wide circulation, even in Protestant America, of a book by a well-known cardinal which reiterates the dogma of papal infallibility and other errors, and which professes to have reached its forty-seventh edition; and also by the wide circulation of the theories of the Tübingen school of critics, through " its small imitators and camp-followers along the byways of popular literature," as to the late origin of the gospels, especially that of John. This demand cannot be met by referring those who have been disturbed by such representations to volu-

minous treatises of a technical character, as all
pastors who have had to deal with active minds
in reading communities well know.   Nor is the
unsuitableness of these elaborate works for general
reading the only reason for their failure to meet
the present need.   Some of the most decisive
facts in the controversies referred to have come
to light since the "standard" works on these
subjects were written.   For instance, it has long
been known that there is in the Vatican at Rome
an ancient marble statue of an eminent Christian
minister, author, and martyr, who was born about
fifty years after the death of the Apostle John,
and who has for centuries been reverenced as one
of the saints in the Roman calendar; but not
until the discovery of his great work entitled
"Philosophoumena; or, Refutation of all Heresies," in 1842 (or, rather, until the publication
of it in 1851), was it known, even to scholars, that
this martyr and saint thus honored by Rome
herself, was, as Dr. Schaff has well said, "an
irrefutable witness against the claims of an *infallible papacy*, which was entirely unknown in the
third century."   And not until that discovery
was made, and others still more recent, such as
Tatian's "Diatessaron" (published in 1888) and
the ancient Syriac version of the gospels (found
at Mount Sinai in 1892), was it known how irre-

sistible was the evidence of the genuineness of the New Testament Scriptures.

These discoveries and others are described in the most interesting manner by Mr. Flournoy in the following pages, and their importance to the cause of truth is pointed out with admirable clearness and force. His "saint with a search-light" is the same whose statue still sits in the Vatican, whose *festa* is still observed on the 22d of August in accordance with the appointment of the Breviary, and whose truthfulness is thus vouched for in the strongest manner by the Church of Rome herself, and the same whose recovered work, "Refutation of all Heresies," demonstrates the absurdity of Rome's claim that there has been a continuous chain of infallible successors of Peter. Taking his stand beside this ancient worthy about the beginning of the third century, Mr. Flournoy shows us that this saint's search-light reveals, in four directions, undeniable evidence that the New Testament came down from apostolic times.

It will be observed, further, that this evidence is not of the subjective and uncertain sort, but external, cumulative, and conclusive. It is presented by Mr. Flournoy in a vivacious and attractive style, without any of the ponderous dullness of the tomes, and yet with careful attention to the reliableness of his authorities and the exactness of his statements. In short, he has written an engaging and instructive book on an important subject, and it is commended to the earnest attention of all who wish to know the truth concerning certain urgent questions of the day.

W. W. MOORE.

TO THE READER

AT the extremity of one of the three slender tongues of a strangely shaped peninsula, which runs out from the shores of Macedonia into the Ægean Archipelago, there rises from the blue water's edge a mountain which is in some respects one of the most remarkable in the world. Mount Athos, with its twenty monasteries, eight thousand monks, and most peculiar rules of celibacy, has been known for ages as the Holy Mountain. With its lofty peak of white limestone piercing the sky, it is the most prominent object in a scene of surpassing loveliness.

Among the vast stores of the relics of early Christian literature in the libraries of these monasteries, some of which date from the time of Constantine, there was found more than fifty years ago a work of great value, written by St. Hippolytus, a man who was born little more than a half-century after the death of the Apostle John. Fresh interest has been created in this book and its author by the recent discovery of another work from the same hand.

An article by Professor George T. Stokes, of

Dublin University, published in the *Sunday at Home*, London, was the means by which the writer's attention was drawn to these discoveries, and he has found the writings of St. Hippolytus to be, indeed, a light shining in a dark place—a veritable search-light on men and affairs in the church in Rome before and after the year 200. In addition to this, they reveal many proofs of the genuineness of the New Testament Scriptures.

The distinguished president of Princeton University, Dr. Francis L. Patton, has lately been quoted as saying that the great question of our times is, What is the Bible? A question of the day scarcely inferior in importance to any other but this one is, What is the papacy? This little volume, it is hoped, will furnish welcome aid to honest inquirers in finding the true answers to these questions.

In pursuing the studies suggested by the article of Professor Stokes just referred to, the author has followed some of the paths along which the light of discovery has fallen, and if he can take others by the hand and show them what has been most interesting and profitable to himself, in such a way as to give them a tithe of the pleasure and benefit which he himself has derived from this pursuit, he will be very thankful.

P. P. F.

BETHESDA MANSE, July 21, 1896.

I

THE MARBLE CHAIR AND ITS OCCUPANT

THE SEARCH-LIGHT OF
ST. HIPPOLYTUS

I

THE MARBLE CHAIR AND ITS OCCUPANT

THERE has been for more than three centuries in the Vatican at Rome the statue of an eminent Christian, who was born about fifty years after the death of the " disciple whom Jesus loved." He was an able and voluminous writer, with keen, clear vision of passing events, and the faculty for portraying them—the ability " to hold, as 'twere, the mirror up to nature; to show virtue her own feature, scorn her own image, and the very age and body of the time, his form and pressure." Hence his account of his own times is very interesting and valuable.

Fifty-four years ago that one of his many books which is probably the most interesting and valuable of them all was recovered after an entombment of many centuries; while quite recently still another long-lost treasure, a product of his pen, has come to light.

The first of these three discoveries is thus described by Dr. Christopher Wordsworth:*

"In the year 1551 some excavations were made on the *Via Tiburtina*, or road to Tivoli, not far from the Church of S. Lorenzo, near Rome. The clearing away of the accumulations of an ancient cemetery and chapel on that site led to an interesting discovery.

"A marble statue of a figure sitting in a chair was brought to light. The person there represented was of a venerable aspect, bald, with a flowing beard, and clad in the Greek pallium.

"The two sides and back of the chair were found to be covered with inscriptions in Greek uncial letters. The right side of the chair exhibits a calendar, which designates the days of the months of March and April, with which the fourteenth day of the moon coincides. This calendar, indicating the paschal full moons, is constructed for seven cycles of sixteen years each, dating from the first year of the Emperor Alexander Severus, which is proved from this calendar to be A.D. 222.

"According to the theory on which the calendar is made, after the completion of one cycle of

* "Hippolytus and the Church of Rome," pp. 42-45.

sixteen years, the full moons recur on the same day of the month, but one day earlier in the week; and the table is formed so as to represent in seven columns the day on which the full moon falls during seven periods of sixteen years.

" The other side of the chair represents a table indicating the day on which the Easter festival falls in each year, for the same period of cycles of sixteen years, dating also from A.D. 222.

" When the fourteenth day of the moon falls on a Saturday then the Easter festival is not to be celebrated on the morrow, or following Sunday, but on the Sunday after that.

" This regulation was in accordance with the Latin practice, but at variance with the Alexandrine custom, according to which the paschal table also is constructed in seven columns of sixteen years each, and indicates the day of the month in which the paschal festival would fall from A.D. 222 to 333.

" Many things in this calendar betoken that it is the work of a Western, and that it was designed for the Western Church.

" The carved back of the chair, which was somewhat mutilated, presents a catalogue of titles of works, composed, doubtless, by the person who occupies the chair.

" This statue thus discovered was in a fragmentary state, but was happily preserved by

Cardinal Marcello Cervino, afterward Pope Marcellus II., and was removed as a valuable monument of Christian antiquity to the Vatican, and was restored by Roman sculptors as far as might be under the auspices of Pope Pius IV."

The questions which naturally occur to us at this point are such as these: Who is the person represented in this statue? In what place did he live? What circumstances called forth the works whose names are inscribed on the back of his marble chair?

As has long been known, this person is Hippolytus, a disciple of Irenæus. Irenæus was himself a disciple of Polycarp. Polycarp, after having served our Lord "eighty and six years," died a martyr's death at Smyrna in A.D. 155.* *He was a disciple of the Apostle John.* Hippolytus, who was himself a martyr, is one of the saints in the Roman calendar, his festa being marked in the Breviary as on August 22d.

About his position in the church there seems to be some divergence of statement, and but little is known of his personal history, owing, doubtless, in part, to the severity of the persecution of the giant emperor Maximin, under whom he suffered. He is often called the Bishop of Portus. " Episcopus Portuensis " is his title inscribed on the base of his statue in the Vatican. Portus

---

* According to latest and best authorities.

Romanus was at the mouth of the Tiber on the northern side, built there as the port of the city which was the mistress of the world—the center of commerce as well as of power—partly because Ostia, the original port on the other side of the Tiber, had become less suitable for this purpose by reason of sand-bars.*

He is also called a presbyter or elder, and again he is sometimes spoken of as a Roman bishop. The disagreement of these statements is doubtless only apparent. In the New Testament the names presbyter (or elder) and bishop are used to designate the same officer—the name elder (*presbuteros*) referring to his *dignity* as a ruler, and the name bishop (*episcopos*) pointing to his peculiar *function* as an overseer in the church. Now it is probable that at the early age at which Hippolytus wrote the scriptural usage was still maintained, and the same person was sometimes called elder and sometimes bishop.†
It has been suggested, as an explanation of the

---

* Says Bunsen: " He was also called the Bishop of the Nations, probably from the fact that, as bishop of the port of Rome, he came in contact with representatives of many nations who landed at or embarked from his city " (" Hippolytus and his Age," vol. iv., p. 25).

† That eminent prelatist, Bishop Arthur Cleveland Coxe, says : " But it seems to me to be based upon the relations of Hippolytus as one of the synod, or ' presbytery,' without consent of which the bishop could do nothing important."

fact that he is sometimes spoken of as a bishop of *Rome*, that, as Portus was the port of Rome and only fifteen miles away, it was natural for those at a distance to think of him as a resident of the imperial city. Whether he resided in Portus or in Rome itself, he was certainly a member of the presbytery, or council of presbyters, of Rome, and a very prominent and influential one.

It is not improbable that he resided first in Portus and then in Rome. His writings, especially the ninth and tenth books of the " Refutation of all Heresies," indicate that he was pastor of a congregation in the city of Rome. The historian Eusebius thus speaks of Hippolytus:* " At the same time Hippolytus, who composed many treatises,† also wrote a work on the Passover. In this he traces back the series of times, and presents a certain canon comprising a period of sixteen years, limiting his computations to the first year of the Emperor Alexander." A list of works of Hippolytus is then given, concluding with one " Against all Heresies." Eusebius adds, " You will find many others still preserved by many."

We know from other sources that Hippolytus

---

* " Hist. Eccl.," bk. vi., chap. xxii.

† Dr. Schaff speaks of Hippolytus as " the most learned divine and most voluminous writer of the Roman Church in the third century " (" Church History," vol. ii., p. 763).

wrote several other books, some of which, in whole or in part, are still extant. Our chief interest now is in the last one here named, and in one not named in this list, but often spoken of by ancient writers, and long known in part from interesting fragments. This last work is a commentary on the Book of Daniel. It was discovered a few years ago by Dr. Basilios Georgiades on the island of Chalce, near Constantinople. It is on many accounts worthy of notice. For instance, " in it Hippolytus quotes the four gospels as being the very words and teaching of Christ." *

The larger part of the work which stands last in the list of Eusebius, that " Against all Heresies," was discovered more than fifty years ago, and its contents are of very great interest. They give such a lifelike picture of the church in Rome of that day, and of persons in connection with it, as can be found nowhere else.†

As Hippolytus proceeds to deal with the heresies of his own times, he lets in some very unwelcome light for those who would have us believe

---

* See article by Professor Stokes in the *Sunday at Home*, London, for May, 1892.

† " In the two last books [i.e., the ninth and tenth of the " Refutation "] we have the narrative of an eye-witness of important events which took place in the second and third centuries after Christ in the Church of Rome—events of which our previous ecclesiastical histories contained no notice " (W. E. Tayler, in " Hippolytus and the Church of the Third Century ").

that the papacy existed from apostolic times. As says Dr. Schaff, "The Roman Catholic Church placed him in the number of its saints and martyrs, little suspecting that he would come forward in the nineteenth century as a witness against her."

It is especially unfortunate for the Church of Rome that after his " Refutation of all Heresies " had been lost he was canonized as a saint. The infallible church, having put him into her Breviary, and having recognized him not only as a saint, but as one of the highest rank,—a martyr too, —now finds him a very inconvenient saint to carry in her calendar in view of the things which he is found to have said about her in her earlier days. The high esteem and reverence in which Hippolytus was held in the Church of Rome is made evident not only by this marble statue,— so skilfully made as to show that it antedates the decline of art at Rome, so carefully restored when recovered from its long entombment in 1551, and honored with a place in the Vatican ever since,—but by the following story of a visit made by Pope Alexander III. to the shrine of St. Hippolytus at St. Denis, to which place his bones had been carried from Rome in the reign of Charlemagne :

"On the threshold of one of the chapels the pope paused to ask whose relics it contained. ' Those of St. Hippolytus,' was the answer. ' Non credo, non credo,' replied the infallible authority. ' The bones of St. Hippolytus were never removed from the holy city.' But St. Hippolytus, whose dry bones apparently had as little reverence for the spiritual progeny of Zephyrinus and Callistus " (" popes " (?) A.D. 197–222) " as the ancient bishop's tongue and pen had manifested toward these saints themselves " (how much this was we shall see presently), " was so very angry that he rumbled his bones inside the reliquary with a noise like thunder. To what lengths he would have gone if rattling had not sufficed we dare not conjecture. But the pope, falling on his knees, exclaimed in terror, ' I believe, O my lord Hippolytus, I believe! Pray be quiet.' And he built an altar of marble there to appease the disquieted saint." *

From this characteristic medieval legend let us turn to the second discovery, which has, so to speak, given voice to this old saint who had been sitting silent for so many centuries in his marble chair.

* Dr. Schaff's " Church History," vol. ii., p. 770.

II
A SEARCH-LIGHT FOUND

II

A SEARCH-LIGHT FOUND

In 1842 M. Villemain, minister of public instruction under Louis Philippe, King of France, sent Minoides Mynas, a learned Greek, to search for literary treasures supposed to be hidden in old libraries in the East. When he returned there was found among the old manuscripts which he brought a book written in Greek with a double title, " Philosophizings; or, Refutation of all Heresies." *

A considerable part of the work was wanting— the second, third, and part of the fourth books; the rest of the ten books remained, and were deposited, with other finds, in the Royal Library of Paris.

In 1851 an English translation was published by Miller at Oxford, and the work ascribed to Origen. This was done, probably, because the

* Φιλοσοφούμενα, ἡ Κατὰ Ἁιρέσεων Πασῶν Ἔλεγχός.

first book had long been known, and in the Bene-
dictine edition had been erroneously accredited
to this father. Scholars very soon discovered
that a mistake had been made, and, following the
lead of Duncker and Jacobi, Bunsen established
the true authorship.

It is useless to weary the reader with the evidence, though the line of argument is comparatively plain and clear. Suffice it to say that the
well-nigh universal verdict of scholars now is that
it is the work of Hippolytus, to whom a book
with this title is ascribed by Eusebius, Jerome,
Photius, and other ancient writers.

The Romanists draw back from this conclusion
for a very transparent reason. It is this: " He
stands out as an irrefutable witness against the
claims of an infallible papacy, which was entirely
unknown in the third century." *

Dr. Döllinger was an exception among Roman
Catholics, and, as is well known, he long ago
(1870) seceded from the papal church on account
of the decree of the Vatican Council on the infallibility of the popes.

Says Dr. Schaff, " Cardinal Newman declares
it to be simply ' incredible that a man so singularly
honored as St. Hippolytus should be the author
of that malignant libel on his contemporary popes,'
etc. But he offers no solution, nor can he.

* Schaff's " Church History," vol. ii., p. 774.

Dogma versus history is as unavailing as the pope's bull against the comet." *

But it is time that we should look into this long-lost book and see what light it throws on that old world in which Hippolytus lived his life of earnest toil. In the earlier books, false and heathenish philosophies are dealt with; hence the appropriateness of the first title, " Philosophizings."

In the later books he treats of heresies among those who professed Christianity, which is implied in the second title, " Refutation of all Heresies." It is made quite plain that most of the heresies sprang either from some form of false philosophy

* " The authorship of Hippolytus is proved or conceded by Bunsen, Gieseler, Jacobi, Döllinger, Duncker, Schneidewin, Caspari, Milman, Robertson, Plummer, Salmon. Cardinal Newman denies it on doctrinal grounds, but offers no solution " (Dr. Schaff's " Church History," vol. ii., p. 762). For the full proof see Bunsen's " Hippolytus and his Age," vol. i., p. 13, and W. Elfe Tayler's " Hippolytus and the Church of the Third Century."

Added to the testimony of scholars ancient and modern, together with the inscription on the back of the marble chair in which the statue of Hippolytus is seated, including the " Refutation " among his other works, we have the testimony of the author himself. In the tenth book of the " Refutation of all Heresies " he uses these words : " My book which treats of the essence of the universe [Περὶ τῆς τοῦ παντός οὐσίας]." The book " On the Universe " is one of those named in the inscription on the back of his chair. This binds the " Refutation " to the occupant of the marble chair with a chain which sophistry will strive in vain to break. There are few books of ancient times the authorship of which is more certain.

or from Judaism.   He seems to consider that the *statement* of these heresies is sufficient for their refutation.   Indeed, he says, " For the opinions of heretics themselves are sufficient for their own condemnation." Hence he refrains almost entirely from argument, and merely presents their views.

With these matters we are not now interested, and can only lament the fact that in the Christian church thus early there was so sad a departure from the faith and practice of the religion of our Lord Jesus Christ.   In view of these facts, we can well appreciate the need and the wisdom of the solemn warnings of Paul and John to the effect that " perilous times " were at hand.   When we see this " hydra-headed heresy," as Hippolytus aptly styles it, and the terrible lapse into ungodly living on the part of those who had departed from the faith, and that under the leadership and protection of the Bishop of Rome, we have before our eyes an object-lesson on the intimate connection between a belief of the truth and godly living, and on the importance of what is so much decried in our day—a creed in accordance with the Scriptures as the necessary norm and inspiration of scriptural holiness of life.

It is in the ninth and tenth books of the " Refutation " that we have this picture of the church in Rome as it then was—a picture whose vividness of delineation reveals the hand of an eye-witness.

III
TWO SPECIMENS OF INFALLIBILITY

III

TWO SPECIMENS OF INFALLIBILITY

LET us see what light is thrown by the occupant of the marble chair on the so-called chair of
Peter at this period.

In the ninth book of the " Refutation of all
Heresies " we find the following account of two
of the contemporaries of Hippolytus, whose names
are in all the catalogues of the popes, both of whom
were canonized as saints, and each of whom re-
ceives in our day the worship of devout Romanists on the day marked as his festa in the Breviary :
" There was a certain man named Noëtus of
Smyrna.* This fellow introduced a heresy taken
from Heraclitus.† A certain man named Epigo-

---

* On Noëtus and his heresy, see Neander's " Church History,"
p. 371 (Rose's translation).

† Heraclitus the Obscure was a Greek philosopher, a native
of Athens, and was born probably in the sixth century B.C. He
taught that, by the operation of a light ethereal fluid, all things,
animate and inanimate, were created. His unintelligible style
and strange views gave him the surname " the Obscure." Hippolytus shows very clearly how the heresy of Noëtus was derived
from the philosophy of Heraclitus.

nus,* who was his agent and scholar, came to sojourn at Rome, and disseminated his odious doctrine. Cleomenes,* an alien from the church both in life and manners, having become his disciple, helped to establish his doctrine.

"At this period Zephyrinus supposed that he governed the church; being an illiterate and avaricious man, [and] being tempted by the offer of gain, he gave permission to those who resorted to Cleomenes to become his scholars. At length, being himself deceived, he fell into the same error in which Callistus—whose life and the heresy invented by him I will soon set forth—was his adviser and associate in wickedness.

"During the succession of these [bishops] this school continued, being strengthened and increased by the coöperation of Zephyrinus and Callistus." †

Now it is to be remembered that Zephyrinus was, according to the catalogues of the popes, the pope at this time. We see, then, what view a most intelligent contemporary held of his infallibility.

Hippolytus continues in a strain which does not at all impress us with his intention to yield implicit obedience to a supreme authority:

* Theodoret also mentions Epigonus and Cleomenes (*ibid.*, p. 371).

† Theodoret represents Callistus as developing the heresy of Noëtus. (See Dr. Salmon's article on Callistus in Smith's " Biographical Dictionary.")

" Yet we never gave place to them [i.e., Zephyrinus and Callistus], but, on the contrary, frequently opposed them and confuted them, compelling them against their inclination to confess the truth. This confession they made at the time through the influence of shame and in consequence of being compelled to do so by the force of truth." This doubtless refers to discussions in the presbytery, or assembly of " the blessed presbyters," of which we shall presently see some accounts. He continues: " But shortly afterward they returned to wallow in the same mire."

Hippolytus proceeds to " set forth the wicked character of their doctrine," and shows us how they adopted the view of Heraclitus and derived from it one of the most wicked of heresies, which was stamped with the name of the second of these ecclesiastics, his followers being called Callistians. He then goes on to give us a lively picture of Callistus, afterward pope and saint, now called Calixtus I. :

" Callistus strengthened this heresy, being a man crafty in wickedness and versatile in deception, aiming at the chair of the episcopate. He stirred up Zephyrinus, an illiterate and unlearned man, unacquainted with ecclesiastical affairs. This person being a receiver of bribes and a covetous man, Callistus led just as he pleased by the influence of his dogmas and unlawful demands. Moreover, Callistus was continually instigating him to introduce strife among the brethren, when Callistus himself afterward managed to allure both parties by wily words to his own side. At one time he would speak the truth to one party, who held sentiments agreeing therewith, and thus deluded them under the pretense of agreeing with them. At another time he would [speak] similarly to those who professed the opinion of Sabellius, whom he displaced when he was able to keep him steadfast; for at the time that Sabellius was exhorted by us he did not show obstinacy; but when he was alone with Callistus he was instigated by him (professing to believe as he did) to incline to the theory of Cleomenes. But he [Sabellius] did not at this time discover his subtlety; but afterward he found it out, as I will briefly relate."

The narrative brings before us a scene in " the assembly " of " the blessed presbyters," in which Hippolytus appears to be on equal terms with Zephyrinus and Callistus, and, indeed, handles them without gloves as he demonstrates the falsity of their teachings on the doctrine of the Trinity.

To throw light on the state of things in the church, Hippolytus gives us a rather startling view of the antecedents of this man who played so strange a part in the ecclesiastical drama enacted in Rome in his day, and the narrative exhibits the doings of a very remarkable saint.   He tells us that he was of the same age with Callistus, and the story is evidently that of an eye-witness of much that is related.

Callistus was a slave in the service of a wealthy Christian, one Carpophorus, "a man of the faith, belonging to the household of Cæsar."   Now we know that at this period slaves were often professional men, authors, or able men in the conduct of great business enterprises.   Not only was this the case among the Greeks and Romans, but the parables of the talents and of the pounds show us that the same state of things was common among the Jews.   Callistus was ambitious to be a business man, and induced Carpophorus to establish in the Piscina Publica, or Fish-market, a bank, of which he was the cashier and general manager. He gathered in much treasure belonging chiefly to Christians, and largely to widows and orphans among them.   They felt very safe about their deposits, for they had unlimited confidence in Carpophorus, whose character was above reproach, and, as Callistus did business under his patronage and authority, they doubtless felt that their means were in as safe a keeping as can be found in this world, where even the heavy gold seems so often suddenly to develop wings and fly away as an eagle toward heaven.

Whether Callistus gambled, or drove fast horses,

or invested too heavily in real estate during some " boom " of those old times, we have no means of ascertaining; but after a time, to the dismay of the depositors, the bank failed. They very naturally appealed to Carpophorus, who, it turned out, had himself been a heavy loser. He immediately proceeds to call Callistus to account. This nimble saint, however, has not allowed the grass to grow under his heels, and Carpophorus is not able to come up with him till he is in the act of fleeing the country. He is on a ship in the harbor of Rome, by Portus Romanus, at the mouth of the Tiber. But it seems that the wind would·not blow to suit Callistus, though he was to be a pope, and before the ship by which he proposed to take a foreign tour got under sail, lo and behold! his master is seen rowing rapidly in his direction. What shall he do? He has to decide quickly, for presently his outraged and too confiding master will be on board. His mind is soon made up, and over the side he goes, and we behold this saintly personage attempting suicide.

But in this decision he was lacking in that infallibility which he was afterward to acquire. The sailors rescued him. Hippolytus tells us that the ferryman, whose boat was in the middle of the river, was slow, and adds, " But the sailors leaped into the boats, and drew him out, unwilling to come, while those on shore were raising a loud

cry."* The result was that the dripping rascal
was soon in the hands of his master. Carpophorus, on bringing the culprit home, subjected him
to a punishment which was both humiliating and
severe. The " Napoleon of finance " was put to
work in the *pistrinum*, or domestic tread-mill,
in the house of Carpophorus.

Subsequently Callistus was found guilty of another crime. " He hurried on their Sabbath to the
synagogue of the Jews, who were congregated
there, and created a disturbance among them."
The disorderly conduct was of so serious a nature
that he was arrested and arraigned before the prefect of the city, Fuscianus.† Not only the Jews,

---

* It requires no violation of probability to imagine that Carpophorus, once the favorite freedman of Marcus Aurelius, and
now a wealthy officer of the imperial household, speeding in his
chariot out of the Porta Portuensis and over the fifteen miles to
Portus, goes first to the home of the pastor of the Christian
church (as he himself was a Christian and the fugitive a nominal
one), and thence in company with him hastens to the piers, where
he learns that Callistus has embarked. The description of the
exciting scene of the arrest indicates that the narrator was a witness of it. The slowness of the ferryman, the plunge of Callistus, the quickness of the sailors, and the unwillingness of the
rescued to be drawn out, together with the " loud cry" from
those on the shore, are all touches which indicate that the writer
heard and saw what he tells of.

† C. Allius Fuscianus became prefect of Rome probably on the
death of Aufidius Victorinus, who was made prefect in 183 and
died in 185. Fuscianus entered on his second consulship in 188.
Marcia, who was at this time all-powerful with Commodus, having all the honors of an empress, except that of having the sacred

but his own master, Carpophorus, testified against him on this occasion.

It would seem as if he had made the plea that the Jews had accused him because he was a Christian, and had endeavored to make out that it was a case of religious persecution.   Carpophorus assured Fuscianus that he was " no Christian [i.e., no true Christian], having made away with a great sum of money of mine, as I will prove." He was scourged and then sent as a convict to a mine in Sardinia.   He was not a sufferer for his Christian faith, as was Hippolytus himself afterward in the same island, but was sent there as a criminal.

fire borne before her, seems to have obtained relief for the Christians exiled and treated as convicts in Sardinia in the year 186. This helps to fix the dates of the occurrences referred to with tolerable accuracy.

IV

A CALM FOR THE CHRISTIANS

IV

A CALM FOR THE CHRISTIANS

THIS was a time of quiet in the church, a calm between terrible storms; and the Christians in the city of Rome seem to have been specially favored.

There had been dreadful persecutions in the reign of Marcus Aurelius, but now Commodus was on the throne and there was peace. This is one of the riddles of history, for Marcus Aurelius, the philosopher, stands among the first of the Roman emperors for high intelligence, probity, and kindliness. Yet under him it is probable that the Christians suffered more severely than under any of his predecessors, at least in the provinces.

Commodus, his son, is described as one of the worst of men, inheriting none of the virtues of his noble father, but in a very large measure the vices of his wicked mother, Faustina. He seems to have been sensual, heartless, and cruel. It is said that his accession to the throne (A.D. 180) was the signal for a series of cruelties, " rivaling, if not surpassing, those of Nero and Caligula." He seemed to gloat on scenes of blood.

Could we have joined the mighty throngs surging amid the temples and monuments and palaces of Rome on the day of some noted contest in the arena, we should have seen strange sights in those times. Passing through the Roman Forum and along streets where on every hand were the most splendid edifices and works of art, the chefs-d'œuvres of the greatest masters, gathered from the collections of conquered cities, we would have seen looming up before us, as we drifted with the human tide, a building which by its grandeur dwarfed all the rest. As we approach the Colosseum, that vastest of theaters, and stand in something like awe as we try to take in its dimensions, the crowd parts and it is whispered that the emperor is coming. Amid the plaudits of the thoughtless multitude the splendid chariot of the youthful heir of Marcus Aurelius drives at full speed, for he is reckless and careless of trampling down those who are too slow to make way. He alights, but, strange to say, does not mount the steps to the emperor's box on the podium. He turns to the arena, and as the ninety thousand spectators that line the tiers, rising one above the other till they reach nearly to the top of the great walls, hail him as Hercules, is armed by his attendants for the combat. Tiger after tiger and lion after lion are let loose to bound upon him, only to fall by the resistless weapons which he wields.*

Presently this grows too tame. The blood of mere beasts will not appease his passion for killing. Men must be sacrificed to amuse him and help him make a Roman holiday. The mightiest men come forth, gladiators trained from their youth for sanguinary contests. One after another sinks under his blows until the greed of this monster in human form is glutted, and his imperial arm is weary taking human life, his choicest pastime.

Now, one would think, there would be persecutions more terrible than those of Nero and Domitian. His father, Marcus Aurelius, the Stoic, with rare self-command and dignity, seemed to make

* " To surprise them [the wild beasts] in their solitary haunts, and to transport them to Rome that they might be slain in pomp by the hand of an emperor, was an enterprise equally ridiculous for the prince and oppressive for the people. . . .

" He styled himself [as we still read on his medals] 'the Roman Hercules.' . . .

" A panther was let loose, and the archer waited till he had leaped on a trembling malefactor. In the same instant the shaft flew ; the beast dropped dead and the man remained unhurt. The door of the amphitheater disgorged at one time a hundred lions ; a hundred darts from the unerring hand of Commodus laid them dead, as they ran raging around the arena. Neither the huge bulk of the elephant nor the scaly hide of the rhinoceros could defend them from his stroke " (Gibbon, vol. i., p. 160).

it his aim in self-discipline to curb and conquer
what is cruel and ignoble in our nature:

> " To let the ape and tiger die,
> And let the *man* be more and more."

He was a man such as few ages have produced
in moral strength and nobility of character, one
of the finest products of that philosophy which
he professed, and this in spite of physical weakness and suffering. Commodus, with the strength
of a Goliath, seems to have combined the fierce-
ness of the tiger with the fatuity of the ape.
Cruel contests in the arena and disgraceful de-
baucheries and bloody tragedies in the palace
occupied his time and his energies, while he left
the affairs of the empire in a large degree to freed-
men and sycophants.*

Yet under the noble father much Christian
blood flowed, and under the despicable son there
was peace and quietness. How this came about
we may never be able fully to explain; but Hippolytus tells us of some facts which make it probable that the relief from persecution in the reign
of Commodus was due, at least in part, to the influence of a person but for whose presence in the
palace of Cæsar Callistus would never have been
Bishop of Rome and would never have had his

---

* Of him and other emperors, Gibbon says, " Secure of im-
punity, careless of censure, they lived without restraint in the
patient and humble society of their slaves and parasites."

name enrolled in the catalogues of the popes and
the calendar of the saints. Marcia, the favorite
concubine of Commodus, bore some relationship
to the Christians. It would seem to indicate a
very low grade of moral sentiment in the church
in Rome at this time if she was a member of it.
Yet this seems to be implied in what Hippolytus
says of her, unless, as some think, his words are
ironical; and it cannot be considered greatly out
of keeping with other facts on which he throws a
surprising light. However this may have been,
the influence of this woman probably stayed the
arm of the bloody tyrant and trifler from descend-
ing on the Christians in the empire.

This may be inferred, for instance, from what
Hippolytus says of the liberation of Callistus:

"Some time after, Marcia, wishing to do a good
work, sent for Victor [then Bishop of Rome] and
asked what Christians had been transported to
Sardinia, adding that she would ask the emperor
to release them; but, being a judicious and righteous man, he omitted the name of Callistus,
knowing the offense he had committed.

"Marcia obtained the letter of pardon, and
Hyacinthus,* a eunuch [of the service of the
palace undoubtedly] and a presbyter [of the
church], was despatched to the governor of the
island to claim and bring back the martyrs.

* Hyacinthus was the foster-father of Marcia.

Hyacinthus delivered his list, and Callistus, finding that his name was not upon it, began to lament and entreat, and at last moved Hyacinthus to demand his liberation also."

So Callistus, the convict, comes back to the scene of his former exploits to perform others, which, though not at all more meritorious than those which sent him a convict to Sardinia, were to elevate him to the bishopric in Rome and to a place in the calendar of the saints.

When he came back to Rome Victor was greatly troubled in view of the scandal which his presence would bring on the church; but, " being a good-natured man," instead of excommunicating him, he only insisted that he should leave the city and live at Antium.

V

THE BANKER MADE A BISHOP

V

THE BANKER MADE A BISHOP

IN the year A.D. 197 Victor died, and Callistus came back to Rome again. Zephyrinus became bishop. Callistus gained great influence over him, as we have already seen. He received from Zephyrinus an appointment, a remarkable memorial of which still exists in Rome. He was placed in charge of "the cemetery" (beautiful name, "sleeping-place") where the bodies of Christians who had "fallen asleep" were laid away to await the call of Him of whom the proclamation has been made, "Behold, He cometh with clouds, and every eye shall see Him," and also, "All them that sleep in Jesus will God bring with Him."

It seems quite probable that the catacomb of St. Calixtus is the same "cemetery" which was used by the Christians at the end of the second century. There is still a pagan tomb of the second century at the entrance to this catacomb, indicating that it was in existence in the days of

Zephyrinus and Callistus, and its interior has been found to be rich in inscriptions, frescos, and other relics of early Christianity.

The combination of avarice and illiteracy in Zephyrinus seems to have suited well the aims and purposes of Callistus. He had long to wait before he could obtain full possession of the object of his ambition, for Zephyrinus occupied the seat he coveted for twenty years (197–217). Yet Callistus seems to have wielded the power of the position without bearing its responsibilities. Taking advantage of the ignorance and venality of Zephyrinus, he seems to have used him as an automaton through whose hands he played his own game and gained his own ends.

This was a sad time for Christianity, in spite of the freedom from persecution; for Zephyrinus was the weak tool of Callistus, the wicked schemer and active promoter of heresy.

When Zephyrinus died, in 217, Callistus, having doubtless thoroughly arranged everything beforehand for this event, and standing by in expectancy, vaulted into the empty seat. The bad banker was now a bishop.

What sort of a bishop will he make? Bad men have become good through divine grace. It is the glory of the Christian religion that it lifts men from the lowest depths of degradation to the loftiest and purest heights of true nobility. But

when a man has lived for a large part of a lifetime
as a professing Christian, and has all along not
only been guilty of foibles and weaknesses, but
has systematically formed and carried out wicked
and selfish designs, we can have but little hope
that any position of responsibility to which he
may attain will work any great change for the
better in his character. In such a case we need
not expect such a transformation as is said to
have taken place when the wild, roistering Prince
Hal became Henry V.

Let us see what a neighboring bishop has to
say of Callistus after he has been elevated to the
bishopric. Our friends of the Church of Rome
would have us believe (especially since 1870) that
he was now a pope with universal and infallible
authority. Of course, then, we should expect
that all other bishops, and especially those whose
lives were such as to gain them the crown of
sainthood, would be found bowing before this
universal father and potentate with all possible
humility, and ready to obey every mandate without a whisper of dissent or protest.

What did Hippolytus think of " Pope " Callistus? Here is what he says: " He was indeed an
impostor and a villain [πανοῦργος], and in the end
drew many after him." This surely cannot be a
pope of whom a Roman saint and bishop thus
speaks!

So much for the character of Callistus; but what of his theology? Hippolytus was a good judge of this. He was a worthy forerunner of Athanasius in the great contest against those of every shade of opinion who taught false views concerning the person of Christ and the doctrine of the Trinity. Hear what he says of this man who was, according to the present teaching of Romanists, the infallible teacher of the church: "Callistus took the lead in propagating this heresy, and devised certain additions to the impiety of the doctrine [i.e., Noëtianism]."

Cardinal Gibbons says:* "What, then, is the real doctrine of infallibility? It simply means that the pope, as successor to St. Peter, Prince of the Apostles, by virtue of the promises of Jesus Christ is preserved from error of judgment when he promulgates to the church a decision on faith or morals."

Now it must be remembered that Callistus is one of the so-called successors of St. Peter. After him several other popes were named, and he is thus an honored link of that unbroken chain of infallible teachers, *every* link of which was stamped "infallible" by the Vatican Council in 1870. How poorly the facts revealed by the search-light of Hippolytus agree with the dogma of infallibility, as thus defined by this notable exponent of

* "Faith of our Fathers," chap x.

Romanism, we have seen and shall see yet more clearly.

Hear Hippolytus again: " The infatuated and tricky fellow, who pours forth blasphemy wherever he goes, . . . and is not ashamed at one time to fall into the dogma of Sabellius, and at another that of Theodotus." Theodotus denied the divinity of Jesus Christ, our Lord, and Sabellius, as is well known, the true doctrine of the Trinity.

Is this an infallible pope, who "is preserved from error of judgment when he promulgates to the church a decision on faith or morals"? Strange light is this which our saint with his search-light sheds on the fabled " chair of Peter "!

VI

POPES (?) AND PRESBYTERS

VI

POPES (?) AND PRESBYTERS

WHILE this manner of speaking on the part of
Hippolytus shows clearly that Callistus was not,
as is claimed by the Roman Catholic Church, a
pope with universal and infallible authority, the
same thing is made perfectly clear by the account
that Hippolytus gives us of a trial for heresy. It
was a *cause célèbre.*

The person charged with heresy was no other
than that Noëtus whose theory of the Trinity
Callistus adopted, adding " to the impiety of the
doctrine." Is the trial according to the papal
system? Let us see. Hippolytus tells us:
" When the blessed presbyters [*makarioi presbu-
teroi*] heard this, they summoned him [Noëtus]
before the assembly and examined him. But he
denied at first that he held such opinions; afterward, however, taking shelter among some, and
having gathered round him some others who had
embraced the same error, he wished thereafter to
uphold his dogma openly as correct. And the

blessed presbyters called him again before them and examined him.   But he stood out against them, saying, ...   And *the presbyters* replied, ...   Then, after examining him, they expelled him from the church, and he was carried to such a pitch of pride that he established a school." *

This school, in which Noëtianism, alias Patripassianism, was taught, survived and was made very influential under Callistus, who made it exceedingly popular by adding the doctrine of " free love," as we shall presently see.

Does not this show that trials were conducted by presbyters sitting as a court?   Is not this very much like a presbytery?   Tayler remarks that already " the fine gold was dimmed."   It was indeed.   *But here we find no pope to make an authoritative decision*, but a body of presbyters. Precisely in keeping with this representation of the mode of ecclesiastical procedure in Rome in the days of Hippolytus is what he says in another place, where Zephyrinus is represented not as the occupant of a papal throne, but as a member of the assembly of presbyters.   In this passage † he says, " Callistus, *putting Zephyrinus forward in the assembly*, persuaded him to say," etc.

Here we have a vivid picture of the great struggle which Hippolytus had with these here-

* Hippolytus against the heresy of one Noëtus.
† " Refutation," book ix., chap. vi.

tics, and this is the occasion on which Zephyrinus, manipulated by Callistus, charges Hippolytus with being a " ditheist."

As we read we find that the latter is upholding the orthodox doctrine of the Trinity as taught a hundred years later by Athanasius, and Callistus is denying the existence of three persons in the Godhead.

We find that when Callistus was charged with teaching that the Father suffered, and upheld what has been called Patripassianism, he would recoil and go to the opposite extreme of denying the divinity of Christ, as Theodotus, who was excommunicated in the time of Victor, had done. In the words of Hippolytus, " Callistus at one time branches off to the opinion of Noëtus, but at another into that of Theodotus, and holds no sure doctrine." *

Thus we find Hippolytus carrying out his intention (expressed in book ix., chap. i.) " to furnish an account and refutation of those heresies *that have sprung up in our day*, by which *certain ignorant* and *presumptuous men* have attempted to *scatter abroad the church*, and have introduced the greatest confusions among all the faithful throughout the entire world."

If Callistus and Zephyrinus were popes with infallibility and universal authority, what are we

* " Refutation," book x., chap. xxiii.

to think of Hippolytus and Athanasius and all the orthodox condemnations of Patripassianism and Socinianism ?

Yet Callistus (Calixtus I.) is in all the catalogues as a pope, and in the Breviary at his name the remark is appended, " Maxima veneratione colitur" ("He is worshiped with the greatest veneration ").

In the light which Hippolytus sheds on the contest in the assembly, and in all that he says of these wicked and blasphemous heresies, is it possible to conceive an absurdity which excels that of the claims of the Roman Catholic Church ?

VII

"THE MYSTERY OF INIQUITY"

"THE MYSTERY OF INIQUITY"

THUS we see how Hippolytus, in the words
of Dr. Schaff, "stands out an irrefutable witness
against the claims of an infallible papacy, which
was entirely unknown in the third century."
It is quite plain that, if Zephyrinus and Callistus were popes, Hippolytus, who surely ought to
have known it, was entirely ignorant of the fact.
Yet what he tells us of another phase of the administration of Callistus shows us that he pretended to grant something very much like the
indulgences of later times, and we find that this
dreadful wickedness aroused indignation and
called forth protests no less earnest and decided
than it did in the sixteenth century. Hippolytus
was not only the Athanasius, but the Luther, of
his time. He is as earnest in opposing Zephyrinus
and Callistus in the year 200 as was Luther against
Leo and Tetzel thirteen centuries later.

Though the papacy was not established at this
time, it is easy to see that *the germs of the ini-
quitous system were developing.* "The mystery
of iniquity," which existed even in Paul's day,

and did " already work," was now growing strong and bold.   Indeed, it would seem that the theory was not now in an early stage of evolution, but had sprung full armed and equipped from the fertile brain of this saint who is still invoked and adored at the altars of Romanism in every land on the fourteenth day of October.

Hippolytus goes on to inform us that Callistus, by the promise that he would forgive sins, encouraged fornication, nameless crimes of lust and uncleanness, and even abortion; allowing the rich to revel in debauchery, and yet providing rules by which they might still remain in good and regular standing in the church; allowing all to come to the communion, and wresting the Scriptures to justify his course.   Hippolytus exclaims: " See to what a pitch of impiety this lawless one [*anomos*] proceeded, teaching fornication and murder at the same time!   Yet, in the face of all these enormities, these men are lost to all sense of shame and presume to call themselves *the Catholic Church.*" *

---

* Tertullian (" De Pudicitia," §1) says, in fine scorn of the pretensions of Zephyrinus or Callistus : " I learn that an edict has been given, even a peremptory edict.   The sovereign pontiff [*pontifex maximus*], that is, the bishop of bishops, has said: ' I remit the sins of impurity and fornication to those who do penance.'   O edict! not less can be done, then, than to ticket it, ' Good work.'   But where shall such an edict be posted?   Surely, I think, upon the doors of the houses of prostitution."

Here we see plainly the beginnings of that long series of pretensions and usurpations of power on the part of a bishop of Rome which finally developed, in A.D. 607, into the full-blown papacy, when the decree of Phocas compelled the submission of other bishops to the Roman see, and the bishops of Rome became popes. But there is not the slightest indication that Hippolytus felt that it was his duty to yield obedience to Zephyrinus or Callistus.

VIII

CALLISTUS AND THE CALLISTIANS

VIII

CALLISTUS AND THE CALLISTIANS

IT is perfectly clear that Hippolytus, so far from acknowledging Callistus as the infallible head of the church universal, indicted him as an arch-heretic, and it is equally clear that this accusation does not apply only to his career before he reached the coveted episcopate, but more especially to his acts and utterances while in that position. He was not only guilty of these things while he was operating his automaton, Zephyrinus, but more flagrantly after he is supposed to have become infallible.

What less than this can be the meaning of such an expression as this? " It was from Callistus his scholars took their appellation, Callistians, so called on account of *him who was their leader.*" That Callistus was not the acknowledged head and teacher of the church universal, but a designing sectary and a base corrupter of morals, is perfectly clear.

The thought that he owed him obedience has evidently never suggested itself to Hippolytus.

73

On the other hand, he feels that it is his bounden duty to expose his errors and oppose his wicked designs.   Hippolytus, though calling himself a presbyter, reckons himself in the true sense " a successor * of the apostles and guardian of the doctrine of the church," and he acts accordingly. He tells us:

" The impostor Callistus, having ventured on such opinions, *established a school of theology in* ANTAGONISM † *to the church*, adopting the foregoing system of instruction.   And he first invented the device of conniving with men in their sensual pleasures, saying that all had their sins forgiven by himself.   For he who is in the habit of attending the congregation of any one else, and is called a Christian, should he commit any transgression, the sin, they say, is not reckoned to him, provided only he hurries off and attaches himself to the school of Callistus.   And many persons were gratified with his regulations, as being stricken in conscience, and at the same time having been rejected for various heresies, while, also, some of them, in accordance with our condemnatory sentence, had been by us forcibly ejected from the church." ‡   This looks much more as if Callistus were pastor of a church—perhaps the oldest church—in Rome, and Hippolytus

* " Refutation," book i., introduction.
† *Ibid.*, book ix., chap. vii.   ‡ *Ibid.*

of another, than as if Callistus were pope, or even diocesan bishop. Hippolytus continues: " Now such disciples as these passed over to these followers of Callistus, and served to crowd his school." And again: "This one propounded the opinion that if a bishop was guilty of any sin, if even a sin unto death, he ought not to be deposed.* . . . And the hearers of Callistus, being delighted with his tenet, continue with him, thus mocking [deceiving] themselves, as well as many others, and crowds of these dupes flock into his school. Wherefore also his pupils are multiplied, and they plume themselves upon the crowds [attending the school] for the sake of pleasures which Christ did not permit. But, in contempt of Him, they place restraint on the commission of no sin, *alleging that they pardon* those who acquiesce [in Callistus's opinions]." Then is given an account of criminal and unnatural practices

---

* " Whosoever shall affirm that the Holy Spirit is not given by ordination, and therefore that bishops say in vain, ' Receive ye the Holy Ghost,' or *that thereby a character* is not impressed, or that he who was once a priest may become a layman again, let him be accursed " (sessio xxiii., caput iv., canon 4, Decrees of Council of Trent).

" . . . Of this the faithful are frequently to be reminded in order to be convinced that, were even the lives of her ministers debased by crime, they are still within her pale, *and therefore lose no part of the power* with which her ministry invests them " (ninth article of creed, Catechism of the Council of Trent, Donovan's translation, published by command of Pope Pius V.).

which is deemed unsuitable for quotation, showing such a state of morals in the Christian church
as makes one shudder to think of. *And these
things were encouraged by Callistus.* What is the
conclusion from all this, from which it is a relief
to turn away as from an unbearable stench?

It would seem that, for all who are not so in-
cased in prejudice as to be absolutely inaccessible
to argument, these facts are sufficient to over-
throw the dogma of an infallible papacy. They
show plainly that there was at this time, at which
it is claimed that an infallible pontiff occupied a
papal throne, no such person in existence, and
that the wicked bishop Callistus, instead of being
the acknowledged head of the universal church,
was a sectary, leading his followers, in despite and
contempt of the authority of the church, into the
wildest heresy and the most infamous antinomianism. And Rome cannot gainsay these facts,
for they are presented by *one whom she has
sainted, and against whose truthfulness it would
be impiety for her to utter a syllable.*

Thus we see that the dogma of infallibility is
an absurdity, and, moreover, that the so-called
chair of St. Peter is a mere figment of a designing
ecclesiasticism. Ah, how our poor world has bled
and groaned under the delusion! Millions have
shuddered at the thought of this mighty power
to punish eternally any opposition to its behests.

It is clear that the chain of infallible authority supposed to lead back to the chair of St. Peter has many missing links. The search-light of Hippolytus reveals its non-existence, in his times at least. As, in the clear radiance thrown on this dark passage, we follow along the track where this chain was said to lie, and find that it is not there, the plain inference is that it is missing all the way back to its pretended source, the chair of Peter. Hippolytus has evidently never heard of Peter as primate and of popes as his infallible successors. Evidently, then, there is no chain and there is no chair of universal and infallible authority. They were manufactured in the papal workshop after the days of Hippolytus.

Thus the " Refutation of all Heresies," while intended for the refutation of the heresies of those early times, refutes also, by the facts which it lays bare, that which has been the arch-heresy of the Christian era, the infallibility and supremacy of the popes.* Could this but be universally

* It has been well said that " by the bull ' ineffabilis ' that pontiff [Pius IX.] has retrospectively clothed the definitions of Zephyrinus and Callistus with infallibility, thus making himself partaker in their heresies " (" Ante-Nicene Fathers," vol. v., p. 159).

Cardinal Gibbons would evidently claim infallibility for the same " definitions." He says : " The Council of the Vatican, in promulgating in 1870 the pope's infallibility, did not create a new doctrine, but confirmed an old one. In proclaiming this dogma, the church enforces as a law a principle which has always existed as a matter of fact " (" Faith of our Fathers," chap. xi.).

known and fully understood in all its bearings, what fetters would be broken, what darkness would be dispelled!   The power of Rome to delude and torture and destroy would be taken away if all could but hear and fully comprehend the words of Hippolytus.

Then we would say, as we look at this old statue, *O mute marble lips, may it soon be true of you, as of the silent heavens, "There is no language nor speech; their voice is not heard;" yet "their sound is gone out into all the earth, and their words to the end of the world."*

IX

THE SURVIVAL OF THE UNFITTEST

IX

THE SURVIVAL OF THE UNFITTEST

THE " good seed " requires " good ground "
and careful culture for its full development; but
ill weeds grow apace without any effort or care.
This Noëtian-antinomian heresy of Callistus grew
and spread after his death in A.D. 222, the year
in which the good emperor Alexander Severus
ascended the throne.   Shakespeare has said most
truly :

" The evil that men do lives after them." *

Oh, that it, instead of the good, could be " in-
terred with their bones " !

It is not strange that multitudes had crowded
to the school of Callistus which he had " established in antagonism to the church."   It was
a very pleasant thing for those who wished
to live in the indulgence of " pleasures which
Christ did not permit " to be informed that this
made no serious difference; that, though Bishop
Hippolytus and the bishops of other congrega-

* " Julius Cæsar," act iii., sc. 2.

tions in the city were so strait-laced and old-fashioned as to exclude them as unfit to be church-members, there was one Bishop Callistus, who would readily forgive their offenses if they would but attend his new theological school. Here there was some scope for breadth and advanced thought. The disagreeable features of the teachings of Christ and the apostles were there smoothed down or eliminated, and a pleasing *liberalism* had taken the place of a crabbed, strict orthodoxy in doctrine and a purely biblical rule of life. Callistianism quite naturally acquired a wide-spread popularity, like Mohammedanism four hundred years later, and Mormonism in our own century, though the scale on which it operated was more contracted than that of Mohammedanism by reason of the true Christianity which surrounded it, and largely through the energy and determined opposition of Hippolytus and his fellow-pastors in Rome.

We have already seen how the "blessed presbyters" began to wrestle with the error at first in order to throttle it in its birth by excluding Noëtus of Smyrna, its originator, from the church. But the wily and able Callistus eluded their vigilance and defied their authority, as he had the crowd, doubtless, of the worldly and the rich at his back, and, instead of being deposed, was made a "saint." His invention of a "second

baptism," by which it was claimed that all sins
were washed away, became specially popular, it
seems; for nothing so pleases those who wish to
live in sin and yet be saved, as an arrangement of
this sort. To such, one work which they can
perform or external ordinance which can be administered to them is more highly prized than all
the truths of Scripture and all the "exceeding
great and precious promises" of the gospel. The
definite "work done" (*opus operatum*) is a
soothing salve for the wounded conscience much
sought after by Christians of this stamp, and the
second baptism of Callistus was just the thing to
meet the popular demands of the unspiritual. It
was "too good a thing" to be allowed to die
with its originator. The antinomianism of Callistus lived after him and gained new vigor. First
connected with Noëtianism by him, it formed a
copartnership after his death with another of the
fantastic heresies of the time.

Hippolytus gives us the sequel of this heretical
movement in the seventh and eighth chapters of
the ninth book of the "Refutation." He had
struggled for twenty years with Zephyrinus and
Callistus united, and then with Callistus invested
with new authority, for five more, against errors
that threatened to destroy the very life of the
church and cover with reproach the very name
of Christian. Now he was becoming Hippolytus

the aged, but he must continue the battle. He and Callistus were, as he tells us, " of the same age." The latter must, then, have been about seventy when he died in 222. Hippolytus, now under the burden of threescore years and ten, must gird on his armor again, for the battle is about to wax hotter than ever. A new and formidable foe appears on the scene, one Alcibiades, who broached a heresy founded on a pretended revelation called the " Book of Elchasai." But let Hippolytus tell the story :

" The doctrine of this one [Callistus] having been noised abroad throughout the entire world, a cunning man and full of desperation, one called Alcibiades, dwelling in Apamæa, [a city] of Syria, examined carefully into this business. And, considering himself a more formidable character, and more ingenious in such tricks than Callistus, he repaired to Rome; and he brought thither some book, alleging that a certain just man, Elchasai, had received this from Seræ, a town of Parthia, and that he gave it to one called Sobiaï. [He alleged] that it had been revealed by an angel whose height was twenty-four *schoenoi*, which make ninety-six miles," etc.

Alcibiades represented that Elchasai's " new remission of sins " had been preached as early as " the third year of Trajan." Hippolytus continues : " And [Elchasai] determines [the nature of] baptism, and even this I shall explain. He alleges [as regards] those who have been involved in every species of lasciviousness and filthiness and [in] acts of wickedness, if only any [of them] be a believer, that he determines that such an one, on being converted * and obeying the book [of Elchasai], should by baptism receive remission of sins.   He, however, ventured on these knaveries, *taking occasion from the aforesaid tenet of which Callistus stood forward as a champion.*

" For, perceiving that many were delighted with this kind of a promise, he considered that he could opportunely make the attempt [just alluded to].

" Notwithstanding, we offered opposition to this [heretic] and did not permit many for any length of time to become victims of the delusion.

" For we carried conviction [to the people when we affirmed] that this was the operation of a spurious spirit and the invention of a heart inflated with pride, and that this [heretic], like a wolf, had risen up against many wandering sheep which Callistus by his [arts of] deception had scattered abroad."

Of this leader of the Elchasaites, or advanced Callistians, Hippolytus tells us : " To those, then,

---

* This " conversion " evidently was the acceptance of Elcha-saism, and had nothing to do with a turning from sin to righteous-ness.

that have been orally instructed by him he dispenses baptism in this manner, addressing to his dupes some such words as the following:

" ' If, therefore, one shall ' "—here are named crimes of the lowest conceivable nature, unsuitable even to mention,—" ' and is desirous of obtaining forgiveness of sins, from the moment that he hearkens to this book [of Elchasai] let him be baptized a second time in the name of the great and most high God, and in the name of His Son, the mighty King, and *by baptism let him be purified and cleansed*, and let him adjure for himself these seven witnesses that have been described in this book—the heaven, and the water, and the holy spirits, and the angels of prayer, and the oil, and the salt, and the earth.'

" These constitute the astonishing *mysteries* of Elchasai and those ineffable and potent secrets which he delivers to his deserving disciples."*

Are the additions which the Roman Catholic Church has made to the simple baptism ordained by Christ survivals of Callistianism and Elchasaism? Rome does, indeed, condemn a *second* baptism; but the efficacy ascribed to the sacrament, the exorcism, the oil and the salt used in administering it, are very suggestive of Elchasai's rite, while the fact that baptism in both cases is called a *mystery* indicates in no uncertain way a

* " Refutation of all Heresies," book ix., chap. x.

connection between what Hippolytus speaks of with disgust and righteous indignation and the Romish ordinance of the present day.

Looking back at this old-time contest between antinomian heresy and true Christianity, one can hardly refrain from joining in the generous outburst of the American editor of the works of Hippolytus (Bishop A. C. Coxe):

" My soul be with Hippolytus when the great Judge holds His assize. His eulogy is in the psalm, ' Then stood up Phinehas, and executed judgment: and so the plague was stayed. And that was counted unto him for righteousness unto all generations forevermore.' " *

* " Ante-Nicene Fathers," vol. v., p. 160.

X
TWO GREAT CHRISTIANS MEET

X

TWO GREAT CHRISTIANS MEET

WE would fain know more of this noble defender of the faith, but the baptism of fire which swept over the Christian church just after the usurpation of the imperial throne by the Gothic giant, Maximin the Thracian, seems to have destroyed almost all personal memorials of his career; but the statue in the marble chair attests the high esteem in which he was held. It presents to us still a form most venerable for age and benign dignity, while the inscriptions upon the chair indicate his participation in the endeavor to settle one of the controversies which for many years divided the church. These inscriptions, as we have seen, also point to some of the many works in which he labored long to maintain and present to the church and the world the great truths of the Scriptures on other points of far greater importance than the timing of the Easter festival.

Though he was threescore years and ten

when the contest with Callistus ended with the
death of the wicked bishop in 222, his work was
not near its completion. In the thirteen or
fourteen years that followed it is not improbable
that much of his literary work, of which many
fragments have come down to us, was done. It
is certain that the great work which was begun
in his student days, and was at first but a synop-
sis of the lectures of his teacher, Irenæus, was
not completed till this period; and in his " Chroni-
cle " is recorded, in what was perhaps one of the
last strokes of his prolific pen, the death of the
good emperor Alexander Severus in A.D. 235.

He wrote commentaries on Genesis, Exodus,
Numbers, the Books of Samuel, the Psalms,
Proverbs, Ecclesiastes, the Canticles, the Greater
Prophets, and Zechariah. That on Daniel, recently discovered, has already been referred to.
He wrote commentaries on books of the New
Testament too, and fragments of those on Matthew, Luke, and the Revelation still exist. He
also wrote a defense of John's Gospel and of the
Revelation. He was one of those to whom God
had given " a banner, that it might be displayed
because of the truth," and very nobly and cour-
ageously did he display it.

When Maximin the Thracian had compassed
the deaths of Alexander and his noble mother,
Mammæa, the guide of his youth, the next vic-

tims of his wrath were the Christians; for they had been favored by Alexander and were attached to him.

In the emperor's youth Mammæa had sent for Origen to come to Antioch, and there listened to his instructions with great interest. In this privilege Alexander was doubtless a sharer.

Eusebius tells us that Origen visited Rome * in the reign of Caracalla (211–217), and, strangely enough, Jerome notes the fact that one of the homilies of Hippolytus shows the presence of Origen when it was delivered.† These two great men, then, seem to have met when Alexander Severus was a youth. Is it not probable that they talked of the hopeful prospect that the future emperor would be a Christian and that the empire might be won for Christ? We cannot know. But it is certain that when Alex-

* According to Eusebius, this visit of Origen to Rome was during the episcopate of Zephyrinus. He says ("Hist. Eccl.," book vi., chap. xiv.): "Origen, . . . while Zephyrinus at this time was Bishop of the Church of Rome" (he does not intimate that this was the church universal), "says that he also came to Rome, being desirous to see the very ancient Church of Rome."

† According to a great scholar (W. E. Tayler, "Hippolytus and the Church of the Third Century," p. 38), "History records that he [Hippolytus] was the first preacher of note in the Church of Rome."

The opinion has been expressed by another equally distinguished student of Christian biography, Dr. Salmon, that Origen probably received a great impetus in his brilliant course from Hippolytus.

ander Severus, who was looked upon as the almost Christian emperor, was slain that the altogether pagan giant, Maximin, might ascend the throne, Hippolytus was among the victims in the persecution which followed.

There must have been much in common between Hippolytus and the brilliant genius and untiring student, Origen. They were both great students of the Word of God, and it is probable that the ardent and enthusiastic younger scholar had not yet mingled with his teachings drawn from the Word of God those unorthodox views which came from the pagan philosophies of the day which Hippolytus so earnestly combats in his " Refutation." At this time Origen must have been engaged in the ardent pursuit of those studies for the more favorable prosecution of which he left Alexandria, the scene of his brilliant success as a teacher in the school established by the great Clement of Alexandria, whom he succeeded when he was but eighteen years old, younger than most of his pupils. His enthusiastic pursuit now was the study of Hebrew. He became the greatest living Hebraist, and his monumental work, the " Hexapla,"—the Old Testament in six versions, arranged in parallel columns,—has been of incalculable help in ascertaining and preserving a pure text of this part of the Word of God. Though so young, his great celebrity, it seems, had induced Mammæa to seek his instructions in the truths of Christianity.

On that occasion when Origen was a hearer of Hippolytus there must have been some communion and interchange of thought between the two greatest Christians in the world, and it surely requires no great stretch of the imagination to picture the younger and the older man leaving the house of God together, walking together along the streets of the splendid and wicked city of the Cæsars, and then seeking some spot where they might be free from the noises of the streets and where they might sit and talk of all the wonderful things that God had done for them in the past, the struggles of the present, and the prospects of the future for that church which Christ died to save and for which they were willing to lay down their lives.

If, leaving the thoroughfares of business, they should have gone up the Capitoline Hill, and have sat together under the Italian sky in some of the gardens about the splendid temples there, or on the steps of that Capitol from which the laws for the world-wide empire emanated, they would have found themselves in the center of a scene whose splendor has perhaps never been equaled. Near by them would be seen the temple of Jupiter Capitolinus, the central shrine of pagan worship. To it came the victorious generals as they returned from conquered nations and provinces to offer thanks and sacrifices and to enrich it with captured wealth and works of art. From this their eyes would naturally turn toward that point on the eastern boundary of the great city, where was the pretorian camp to which Paul was brought a prisoner, and where, though himself a captive, he led many a soldier captive in the sweet bonds of Christ's love, preaching to him the glorious gospel of Christ, as the guard and the prisoner lay chained together through the long watches of the night. North of them would be seen the whole length of the Flaminian Way, the finest street in Rome, running parallel to the modern Corso from the Capitoline Mount to the Flaminian Gate on the northern boundary, spanned by the triumphal arches of Claudius and of Marcus Aurelius. To the west of this lay the Campus Martius with all its objects of interest. Toward the setting sun would be seen the Flaminian Circus and the Portico of Octavius. Near the Pantheon would be seen that magnificent bridge erected by Hadrian to lead to his mausoleum, which is still standing under the name of Castle of St. Angelo. A little west of south was the great Circus Maximus, capable of holding three hundred and eighty-five thousand spectators of the chariot-races. This helps us to form some idea of the size of the city of Rome.

On the southeast was the great Cælian Hill, covered with the palaces of men whose income was, in some cases, a large part of the tribute of a conquered province.*

But the splendor of the Italian sky and of the imperial city would not long hold the gaze of two such men in such a time. They might both look toward the Palatine bridge not far away, and then to the more distant Porta Portuensis, as this was the way to Portus Romanus, where Origen may have landed in coming to Rome, and where Hippolytus, as Bishop of the Nations, once exercised oversight for the Christian community, which must have been a veritable "church of the strangers," as Christians from all nations under heaven would land there on their way to Rome. But no earthly sights or sounds could long occupy two minds so full of higher things. Both would naturally think of the terrible persecutions of Septimius Severus, which had ended with the emperor's death in 211. These persecutions had been especially severe in Alexandria, the home of Origen's childhood and youth.

The young man would naturally tell the older of that noble Christian father of his, Leonides, who, being one of the most prominent and devoted among the Christians, was among the first

* On the Rome of the period, see Lord's " Old Roman World " and Ginn's " Classical Atlas."

to be seized in the Septimian persecution. He would gladly have laid down his own life with that of his father, and everywhere proclaimed himself a Christian; but the Lord had work for him, and he was not slain. His pupils were taken, and he did not hesitate to minister to them and to accompany them to the stake; but when his father was arrested a stratagem dictated by a mother's love detained the enthusiastic and devoted boy savant at home, and he could only write to his father urging him to be "faithful unto death." His best scholars were martyred, and he was stoned in the streets and continually in peril of his life; but none of these things moved him. As soon as there was a lull in the tempest he went on teaching again. He could not help speaking to Hippolytus of scenes of such absorbing interest from which he had not long before come. Possibly, too, the memorable conferences with Mammæa and her noble boy had just taken place, and would afford matter of much interest to both talkers.

Then Hippolytus might naturally be reminded of his own youth, and tell Origen of his great teacher, Irenæus. What a wonderful teacher he was! How he clung to the Word of God in the Old and New Testaments at a time when the religious atmosphere seems to have been so charged with heathen philosophies of one kind and another that few could escape the influence of the spiritual malaria! But I think Hippolytus would have dwelt most lovingly on the personal reminiscences which his teacher, who had gone to his rest some twelve or fifteen years before, must often have related to him of a teacher at whose feet he himself had sat in youth—Polycarp, the pupil of John, the beloved disciple of our Lord.

Irenæus, doubtless, often told Hippolytus, as we know he told Florinus, of the times when he was "yet but a boy." He must have spoken much more fully and freely to his beloved pupil, too, than he did to the latter. In writing to the erring Florinus, and in order to induce him to cleave to the truth, he speaks of Polycarp, whom Florinus had known, as follows:

"For I remember the events of those times better than the events of recent occurrence, as the studies of our youth growing with our minds become one with them; so that I can tell the very spot where the blessed Polycarp, being seated, used to discourse, his outgoings and his incomings, his manner of life, the form of his body, his conversations with the people, and his familiar intercourse with John, as he was accustomed to tell, as also with the others who had seen the Lord. How, also, he used to relate their discourses and what things he had heard from them concerning the Lord; also concerning His miracles and His doctrine. All these were told by Polycarp in consistency with *Holy Scripture*" (see how Irenæus speaks of the Gospels), "as he had received them from those who had been eye-witnesses of the life of the Word. These things, by the mercy of God and the opportunity then afforded me, I attentively heard, noting them down not on paper, but in my heart; and these same facts I am always in the habit of recalling faithfully to mind."*

Then Hippolytus would naturally come back from the golden past to the struggles of the present. Here in Rome the Christians highest in authority presented a great contrast to "that blessed and apostolic presbyter," Polycarp, as Irenæus calls him in the same letter. At this time Zephyrinus and Callistus were in full career and the faithful and true were mourning. This was in the time of Caracalla, and, in spite of the fact that this emperor was so bloodthirsty as to slay twenty thousand at one time of those who had adhered to his brother Geta, and to cause a general slaughter of the inhabitants of Alexandria, it seems that the Christians were not persecuted. Elagabalus (or Heliogabalus), the fantastic, effeminate, and pleasure-loving youth who next wore the purple, the Sardanapalus of Rome, who was so reckless of human life and so destitute of

---

* See letter to Florinus, preserved in Eusebius's "Hist. Eccl.," book v., chap. xx.

respect for age or eminence that he is said to have invited the patricians of Rome to a banquet, and while they were at table had the doors opened to let in tigers and bears to tear them limb from limb, seems yet not to have disturbed the calm which the Christians enjoyed. The peace of religion lasted, it seems, through the thirteen or fourteen years of Alexander's reign. But a great change came when he and Mammæa were murdered, as it is supposed, by the contrivance of Maximin, the gigantic Thracian. The giant is said to have consumed forty pounds of meat in a day, washing it down with an amphora of wine, and to have worn his wife's bracelet as a finger ring. Alexander favored the Christians. The bloody ogre vented his fury upon them, taking the bishops first.

Hippolytus was one of the shining marks in the Christian church at which this cruel archer aimed. Both Hippolytus and Pontianus (so-called pope of the time) were sent to the mines of Sardinia. At fourscore the life of a convict could not be very long continued there. Both perished, we know not in what way, and, according to the Liberian Catalogue, both were buried on the same day, Pontianus in the Cemetery of St. Calixtus, and Hippolytus on the Via Tiburtina, where his statue in the marble chair was found in 1551.

The story of Prudentius that Hippolytus was

dragged to death by wild horses in the streets of Ostia is thought to be apocryphal; but it seems probable that both of these men died violent deaths from the fact that both were buried on the same day and that both were enrolled as martyrs. There seems to be a pathetic reference to his own banishment in a fragment of Hippolytus. Addressing the beloved disciple, he says: " Tell me, blessed John, apostle and disciple of the Lord, what didst thou see and hear concerning Babylon? Arise and speak, for it sent *thee also* into banishment." The words seem to have been written during his own banishment.

XI

THE SEARCH-LIGHT AND THE CANON; OR, HOLY SCRIPTURE BEFORE POPES AND COUNCILS

XI

THE SEARCH-LIGHT AND THE CANON; OR, HOLY SCRIPTURE BEFORE POPES AND COUNCILS

THE account given by Hippolytus of the Christian church shows plainly the falsity of the claim of the Church of Rome to a line of infallible popes leading back to Peter. His works show with equal clearness the falsity of the claim that the Roman Catholic Church made up the *canon of Scripture and thus gave it authority by its imprimatur.*

Should this language seem too strong, I will willingly substitute for it that of Cardinal Gibbons, as found in " The Faith of our Fathers " (44th ed., 1894), chapter viii.: " The Catholic Church, in the plenitude of her authority, in the third Council of Carthage (A.D. 397) separated the chaff from the wheat, and declared what books were canonical and what were apocryphal." On the same page he adds, " Indeed, when you accept the Bible as the Word of God, you are obliged to receive it *on the authority of the Catho-lic Church,*" etc.

Now, long before this Council of Carthage, lived Hippolytus. After his active life began *more than two whole centuries* rolled away before this council assembled in the old African city. How was it with the canon two hundred years before this body of men are said to have manufactured it? Bunsen says:

" The whole [New Testament] canon of Hippolytus may be therefore reconstructed thus. It contained:

" (1) The four Gospels.

" (2) The Acts. . . .

" (3) The Pauline epistles to seven distinct churches; nine epistles as we read them. . . .

" (4) The four Pastoral Letters: to Philemon and Titus, and the two addressed to Timothy.

" (5) The six catholic (or general) epistles: the Epistle of St. James; the Epistle of St. Peter (our first); the three epistles of St. John; the Epistle of St. Jude.

" (6) The Epistle to the Hebrews. . . .

" (7) The Apocalypse of St. John." *

It is remarkable that Bunsen represents Hippolytus as omitting the Second Epistle of Peter. This is evidently an oversight, as Hippolytus quotes it several times, and it is once quoted in

* Bunsen, " Hippolytus and his Age," vol. ii., p. 139.

one of the extracts from the "Refutation" in these pages. The reference to Zephyrinus and Callistus as "returning [after an apparent temporary reformation] to wallow in the same mire" is from 2 Peter ii. 22 : "The dog is turned to his own vomit again ; and the sow that was washed to her wallowing in the mire." This is, then, precisely *our* canon of the New Testament.

As to his conception of the *authority* of the Scriptures, Hippolytus views it just as Protestants do. Bunsen does not go at all beyond what any one reading the works of Hippolytus can see to be the fact when he says, "The expressions of Hippolytus on the paramount authority of Scripture in all matters of faith and doctrine are as strong as those of the Reformers." *

If space allowed, abundant quotations from Hippolytus could be cited to substantiate this, but one is sufficient:

"There is one God, my brother, and *Him we know only by the Holy Scriptures*. For, in like manner as he who wishes to learn the wisdom of this world cannot accomplish it without studying the doctrines of the philosophers, thus all those who wish to practise the divine wisdom will not learn it from any other source than from the *Word of God*. Let us, therefore, see what the Holy Scriptures pronounce, let us understand

* "Hippolytus and his Age," vol. ii., p. 144.

what they teach, and let us believe as the Father wishes to be believed, and praise the Son as He wishes to be praised, and accept the Holy Spirit as He wishes to be given. *Not according to our own will, nor according to our own reason*, nor forcing *what God has given;* but let us see all this as He has willed to show it by *the Holy Scriptures."*

This is pure Protestantism, equally free from the spirit of popery, on the one hand, and from unbelieving rationalism, on the other.

Could the grand old champion of a pure Christianity rise and live again on earth, where the two great divisions of those who bear the name of Christians stand opposed, one bearing on its banner, " *The pope, the only infallible teacher,"* and the other the immortal words of Chillingworth, " *The Bible, the Bible alone, is the religion of Protestants,"* there is no doubt as to which ranks the old hero would join. With the prayer that " all may be one," both he and we would rejoice to see unfurled the banner from which should shine forth, " *The Bible, the Bible alone, the religion of all Christians."*

For those Christians whose minds have been disturbed by the representations of the Tübingen school, and its small imitators and camp-followers along the byways of popular literature, as to the probability of the late origin of the Gospels, and especially that of John, it is reassuring to find, in the works of a man born about fifty years after John's death, quotations from all the Gospels and all the other books of the New Testament, and to find also that these writings are continually called " the Holy Scriptures " and " the Word of God."

As to Baur's theory that the Gospel of John was written A.D. 160–170, it is instructive to find Hippolytus, who was a theological student about A.D. 170, speaking in this way about it : " These things, then, brethren, are declared by the Scriptures; and the blessed John, *in the testimony of his Gospel*, gives us an account of this economy and acknowledges this Word as God when he says : ' In the beginning was the Word, and the Word was with God, and the Word was God.' " *

It is still more reassuring to find that the *teacher* of Hippolytus quotes the New Testament in just the same way—as " the Word of God."

The following extract, while very interesting as one of the earliest accounts of the writing of the New Testament, is especially so as showing how the teacher of Hippolytus regarded these writings. He says :

" Matthew also issued a written Gospel among the Hebrews in their own dialect, while Peter and Paul were preaching at Rome and laying the foundations of the church.

* Treatise against the heresy of one Noëtus, §14.

" After their departure Mark, the disciple and interpreter of Peter, did also hand down to us in writing what had been preached by Peter. Luke also, the companion of Paul, recorded in a book the Gospel preached by him. Afterward John, the disciple of the Lord, who also had leaned on His breast, did himself publish a Gospel during his residence at Ephesus in Asia.

" These have all declared unto us that there is one God, Creator of heaven and earth, announced by the law and the prophets, and one Christ, the Son of God. If any one do not agree to these truths he despises the companions of the Lord; nay, more : he despises Christ Himself, the Lord ; yea, he despises the Father also; and stands condemned, resisting and opposing his own salvation, as is the case with all heretics." *

" When, however, they are confuted from *the Scriptures*, they turn and accuse these same Scriptures as if they were not correct nor of authority," etc. †

Irenæus may have been liable, as all men are, to make mistakes in his statements of facts; but there can be no mistake about the fact that the teacher of Hippolytus held the New Testament to be the Word of God and that to reject it was to forfeit salvation.

---

* " Adv. Hæres.," book iii., chap. i.
† *Ibid.*, chap. ii.

According to Keith,* Irenæus, in that part of his works which is still extant (and we have only a part of what he wrote), quotes the New Testament seven hundred and sixty-seven times, and "Irenæus shows throughout his works an intimate knowledge of the Gospels, Acts, and epistles." He quotes the books of the New Testament as "the divine Scriptures," "the divine Oracles," "the Scriptures of the Lord."

The fact that two books of the New Testament, the Third Epistle of John and the Epistle of Jude, are not quoted in the extant writings of Irenæus is no indication that these books were not in the New Testament at that time. For we find that these two epistles together contain only thirty-nine verses, and any of us might write twice as much as we have from Irenæus without having occasion to quote either of these very short letters. Indeed, it is a remarkable proof of the importance which he attached to the New Testament that there are found in his writings quotations from all the books of which it is composed, with this exception.

Pothinus was Bishop of Lyons, and suffered martyrdom there in A.D. 177 in a most ruthless persecution under Marcus Aurelius. Irenæus, who had been associated with him in his labors in Gaul, was made bishop in his stead, and seems

* "Demonstration of the Truth of Christianity," chap. vi.

not to have hesitated to assume the duties of a position than which none could have required more courage and stronger faith.

A letter was written by the churches, and probably sent by Irenæus, who was in Rome the following year, addressed "to those brethren in Asia and Phrygia having the same faith and hope with us." Asia was the name of a small division of the region afterward called Asia Minor, and Ephesus was its capital. This was the scene of the last days of the Apostle John, and the letter, while telling of the inhuman tortures and deaths of various members of their churches, dwells upon the suffering and faithfulness unto death of the aged and beloved bishop Pothinus. These facts certainly involve a strong probability that Pothinus, like Polycarp, was a disciple of John.

After describing the fiery trial and glorious triumph of others who laid down their lives for Christ, the letter continues: "But the blessed Pothinus, who had faithfully performed the ministrations of the episcopate at Lyons, and was past his ninetieth year and very infirm in body . . . when carried by the soldiers to the tribunal, and when the mob raised a cry against him, gave a noble testimony. When asked by the governor, 'Who was the God of the Christians?' he said, 'If thou art worthy thou shalt know.' After this he was unmercifully dragged away, and endured many stripes, while those that were near abused him with their hands and feet in every possible way, not even regarding his age. But those at a distance, whatever they had at hand every one hurled at him. . . . Thus, scarcely drawing breath, he was thrown into prison, and after two days he there expired." *

In this letter there are quotations from the epistles to the Romans, Philippians, 1 Timothy, 1 Peter, Acts, Gospels of Luke and John, and the Apocalypse. Within the limits of the letter twelve books of the New Testament are referred to. Would a letter of the same length written by Christians in our time, with the whole New Testament before them, be likely to contain more quotations from it if the letter were a narrative of passing events and not a doctrinal discussion? These people in 177 show themselves to have been exceedingly familiar with the New Testament and to have relied on its teachings as their source of instruction and comfort in times when each was liable to those tortures and that death by which their companions had shown their faith in its truths. But this New Testament had been the text-book from which Pothinus had taught them and doubtless the fathers of many of them. Polycarp of Smyrna had sent Irenæus to his aid in his old age. Is not this another indication of

* Eusebius, " Hist. Eccl.," book v., chap. i.

the fact that Pothinus was from Asia? But would Pothinus, who must have been born before the last book of the New Testament was written, have taught it, and died for it, and exhorted his people to die for it, if he had not known that it was written by John? In the letter of the churches of Lyons and Vienne these writings are quoted as " Scripture."

Irenæus was the younger colleague of and co-laborer with Pothinus, and Pothinus was old enough to have sat as a catechumen under the instruction of the beloved disciple. And in the extant writings of Irenæus we have quotations from all the New Testament books, except the thirty-nine verses which make two very short letters. But Irenæus was the disciple of Polycarp, and Polycarp was not only old enough to be, but certainly was, the disciple of John.

Does Polycarp, who sat at the feet of the beloved disciple, indicate in any way the existence of the writings which we call the New Testament? If so, there can be no reason to doubt that they belong to the apostolic age, and that they were written by the persons whose names they bear and to whom they have always been ascribed. With the Apostle John as his instructor, he would certainly have been liable to no possibility of mistake on this point. We have only one piece of writing from Polycarp, his Epistle to the Philippians; but this is of immense value. That doubting Thomas among the critics, Professor A. Harnack, who seems to linger on the edge of a decision in favor of the genuineness of any ancient document confirming the New Testament Scriptures, till absolutely forced over by unquestionable facts, joins his voice in favor of the genuineness of this letter of Polycarp. He says of it that " the external evidence is as strong as could be desired "; and also, " but the internal evidence is also very strong." Of its character he remarks that its " tone, language, and tendency " are " not in keeping with the Ignatian epistles." Of Polycarp he says that he " lived wholly in the ideas of the older generation and of the apostles, and *would admit no addition to their teaching.*" Harnack considers this epistle " of great value for the history of the canon."

In this letter, which is by no means long, Polycarp quotes fifteen books of the New Testament, and some of them several times—the Gospel of Matthew, for instance, if I mistake not, *ten times.*

Now, if there had been any doubt in the mind of Polycarp about the genuineness of these writings, would he have written a letter saturated through and through with New Testament thought and actually made up in large part of its very language? If they had been forgeries, would Polycarp, the pupil of John, and *his con-*

temporary for almost forty years, have quoted them at all?

The very way in which he quotes the New Testament is a clear indication of his reception of it as of divine authority. But he does not leave us simply to infer this, as no one can avoid doing if he reads the epistle. In quoting Ephesians iv. 26 he says, " As it is said in those *Scriptures,* ' Be ye angry, and sin not, and let not the sun go down on your wrath.' "

Thus we find Hippolytus, through Irenæus, his teacher, in whose footsteps he so closely followed in his " Refutation of all Heresies," linked with the apostolic age through these two venerable men, Pothinus and Polycarp, both of whom laid down their lives for the faith which they professed.

When we find Hippolytus, then, with all his means of information, quoting every book of the New Testament, we may feel very sure that those who deny the genuineness of these Scriptures do so in the face of incontrovertible evidence.

When men deliberately lay down their lives rather than deny what they have asserted we have the highest order of testimony to their sincerity in making those assertions. It would be hard to find an exhibition of more thorough sincerity in all history than that of these two witnesses to the truth—Polycarp, the preceptor, and Pothinus, the aged colleague of Irenæus in his ministry in Gaul. The testimony of both has been preserved by letters of the churches which they served.

The church of Smyrna, of which Polycarp was the bishop or pastor, that " angel of the church in Smyrna" addressed by John in the Revelation (or his successor), has left on record the good confession of him who was its guide by his example as well as his teaching for many years. The testimony of Polycarp in his life and in his death was of no ordinary importance. It came at a most critical period, as the seven messages to the churches recorded in the second and third chapters of the Book of Revelation clearly indicate, and such glimpses as we have of the times of Polycarp serve to emphasize this fact.

Says Canon Westcott: " In one respect the testimony of Polycarp is more important than that of any of the apostolic fathers. Like his master [John], he lived to unite two ages; he had listened to St. John and he became the teacher of Irenæus. In an age of convulsion and change he stands at Smyrna and Rome as a type of the changeless truths of Christianity. In his extreme age he taught that which he had learned from the apostles and which continued to be the tradition of the church. . . . Thus the zeal of Polycarp watches over the whole of the most critical period of the history of Christianity. His words are the witnesses of the second age." *

How he loved the truth and hated error, which was becoming so rife in his old age, we are shown by his stopping his ears when the vagaries of Valentinus and of Marcion were urged upon his attention, lamenting the fact that he had been preserved to old age to hear such things.

In character he seems to have been strikingly like his master, John. When he went to Rome to confer with Anicetus, the senior pastor there (whom the Romanists represent as the pope of the time), about the time of the Easter celebration, though he was unable to effect a reconciliation between the advocates of the Eastern and those of the Western churches, there was no breach of charity, and he celebrated the Lord's Supper in Rome, using the Greek language. But, though so loving toward even those brethren who differed from him in such a matter, he was a very Boanerges when the vital truths of Christianity were assailed by heretics.

Marcion seems to have endeavored to approach him, during this visit to Rome, to curry favor with him and secure the powerful aid of his influence; but he was rebuffed with such a lightning stroke as this:

MARCION: " Thou knowest us."

* Westcott on the Canon, p. 40.

POLYCARP: "I know thee as the first-born of Satan."

But his Christian constancy and fortitude were to have a severer test than was afforded by this encounter with the enemies of the faith in Rome.

"The proconsul of Asia Minor [at this time] does not appear to have been personally hostile to the Christians; but the heathen people, with whom the Jewish rabble joined themselves, were enraged against them, and the proconsul yielded compliance to the fury of the people and the demands of the law. . . .

"When he [Polycarp] heard the cry of the people who were eager for his blood, his first impression was to remain in the town, and to await God's pleasure in the event; but the prayers of the church prevailed on him to take refuge in a neighboring country-seat. Here he remained in company with some friends, busied day and night, as he was accustomed, in offering prayers for all communities in the whole world.

"When he was searched for he betook himself to another country place, and he had scarcely gone before the police appeared, to whom the retreat of Polycarp had been made known by some confidential but unworthy friends. They found two slaves, one of whom, under the pain of torture, betrayed the place to which the bishop had fled. When they came Polycarp, who was in the upper story, might have retreated from the flat roof to another house, a convenience which the Eastern mode of building afforded, but he said, 'God's will be done!'

" He came down to the police officers, and ordered them as much refreshment as they might be inclined to take, begging only as a favor that they would allow him one hour's undisturbed prayer. The fullness of his heart, however, carried him on for two hours, and even the heathen were touched at the sight of his devotion.

" When this interval had passed he was conducted on an ass to the town, where the chief officer of police, going with his father out of the town, met him, and, taking him into his carriage, spoke to him in a kind and friendly manner. 'What harm,' said he, 'can it be for you to say, " Our lord the emperor "?' Polycarp at first was silent, but when they continued to press him he calmly said, 'I will not do what you advise me.' When they saw that they could not persuade him they grew angry. With bitter and contumelious expressions they threw him out of the carriage so roughly as to injure one of the bones of his leg. He turned and went on his way as if nothing had happened.

" When he appeared before the proconsul the latter said to him, 'Swear, curse Christ, and I will set you free!'

" The old man answered, ' Eighty and six years have I served Him, and I have received only good at His hands! Can I, then, curse Him, my King and my Saviour ? '

" When the proconsul continued to press him Polycarp said, ' Well then, if you desire to know who I am, I tell you freely, *I am a Christian.*' . . . After the governor had in vain threatened him with wild beasts and the funeral pile, he made the herald publicly announce in the circus that Polycarp had confessed himself a Christian. These words contained the sentence of death against him. The people instantly cried out, ' This is the teacher of atheism, the father of the Christians, the enemy of our gods, who has taught so many not to pray to the gods and not to sacrifice!'

" As soon as the proconsul had complied with the demand of the populace that Polycarp should perish on the funeral pile, Jew and Gentile hastened with the utmost eagerness to collect wood from the market-places and the baths. When they wished to fasten him with nails to the pile the old man said, ' Leave me thus, I pray, unfastened. He who has enabled me to abide the fire will give me strength also to remain firm at the stake.'

" Before the fire was lighted he prayed thus: ' O Lord, almighty God! the Father of Thy beloved Son, Jesus Christ, through whom we receive a knowledge of Thee! God of the angels and of the whole creation, of the whole human race, and of the saints who live before Thy presence! I thank Thee that Thou hast thought me worthy, this day and this hour, to share the cup of Thy Christ among the number of Thy witnesses!'"*

Thus was the faithful testimony which Polycarp had borne to Christ through his long life of service crowned and perfected in his death.

Pothinus and Polycarp, to use an expression which Professor Gildersleeve has applied to Justin Martyr, were "no holiday Christians." They *believed* and therefore spoke; for they were willing to seal their testimony with their blood. "All that a man hath will he give for his life." If the New Testament writings had been forgeries these men could not have failed to know it. Polycarp must have been born before most of Paul's epistles were written, and was probably between thirty and forty years old when John wrote his Gospel. It has been made almost certain within the last few years that his martyrdom took place not at the date given by Eusebius, but under the proconsul Quadratus, and on the 23d of February, A. D. 155.† Then he was old enough to say, " Eighty and six years have I served Him."

Pothinus was a contemporary of John for eleven

---

* Neander, "Ch. Hist.," pp. 64, 65, Rose's trans.
† Adolph Harnack.

or twelve years, and Polycarp for *thirty-nine years*, if he dates his service from his tenth year.

Now when we find in the letter of the churches which Pothinus had instructed for so many years, quotations from or allusions to some twelve books of the New Testament, and then turn to the epistle of Polycarp and find it made up in large part of quotations from the New Testament, we may feel sure that we have traced these writings back to the age of the apostles, and that they could not have been written by any persons but those to whom they are ascribed; for these men were in a position to *know* that they were genuine. That they knew it is attested by the fact that they not only taught the truths contained in these writings during their lives, but laid down their lives in attestation of the truth of their teaching.

XII

THE SEARCH-LIGHT ON THE HERETICS

XII

WE know, then, that the assertion of Baur and the Tübingen school to the effect that the Gospels, and especially the fourth Gospel, originated long after the deaths of their reputed authors is absolutely false. The assertion was made and has been maintained to uphold the theory of theological " tendency " evolved out of the fertile, German-student, inner-consciousness of Baur, and is in the face of all the facts of the case. If we had no other proofs of the origin of the Gospels in the apostolic age than these simple facts, that Hippolytus quotes every book of the New Testament as Holy Scripture, that Irenæus before him quotes every book, with the exception of two short letters, containing together thirty-nine verses, that Polycarp, born near the time of Paul's death and for nearly forty years contemporary with the Apostle John, quotes thirteen books of the New Testament in his letter to the Philippians, quoting very much more in proportion to the length of the production than Hippolytus and Irenæus, and that both he and Pothinus, the co-laborer of Irenæus, laid down their lives in attestation of their testimony—these facts alone would be amply sufficient to establish the genuineness of these writings.

Mathematical demonstration is impossible in this, as in all similar cases, but moral certainty is reached from these facts alone. These, however, are far from being the only facts to which Hippolytus introduces us by which the genuineness of the New Testament Scriptures is proved.

Hippolytus, clasping hands with his preceptor, Irenæus, who brings us to Polycarp, thus, through this line of his spiritual ancestry, leads us back to that disciple who leaned on the bosom of the Saviour.

But there is another line to which he introduces us, and by this, as well as by that of his spiritual ancestry, we are led back to John. He introduces us, in his " Refutation of all Heresies " especially, to numerous heretics ; and these bear witness to the existence of the New Testament writings in their day. This testimony has at least one point of special value : it is the testimony of enemies.

This gives us one advantage. We may be sure that when they quote the books of the New Testament these books are not only in existence,—of this their quoting them is evidence,—but that they are already *of recognized authority*, and must have been in existence for a considerable time in order to have been disseminated among all Christians and established in their confidence as the source of decisive authority in religious questions. Had they not been thus disseminated and received as the Word of God among Christians in various countries, these heretics would not have appealed to them as they did.

Let us take a brief glance at some of the heretics to whom Hippolytus introduces us. Without noticing to any great extent their peculiar tenets, matters which are of little interest now, we may with profit notice their treatment of the New Testament Scriptures.

The Ophites, called so because of their theories about the serpent as the Logos, or Eternal Wisdom, formed a sect which existed very early. They are described by Irenæus as well as by Hippolytus, and seem to have existed as a Christian sect from the earlier part of the second century. They represent one branch of the Gnostic heresy, if not the main trunk of it.

" The manner in which they used the New Testament in order to support their special theory concerning the serpent is very curious. They discovered the serpent in the most unexpected quarters, for they used a method of arbitrary interpretation which will enable a man with luxuriant imagination to prove any doctrine from any text. *They quoted the four Gospels, but especially the Gospel of St. John."* *

This sect seems to have combined some of the peculiarities of the Basilidians and Valentinians.

Basilides is said to have been a younger contemporary of the beloved disciple. This is probable, for several authorities represent him as teaching in Rome in the reign of Hadrian (117–138). He quoted the New Testament, and especially the fourth Gospel.

Says the author of the article on Basilides in Smith's " Dictionary of Christian Biography," " In spite of his peculiar opinions, the testimony of Basilides to our ' acknowledged books,' as given by Hippolytus, is comprehensive and clear."

Hippolytus deals with Valentinus and the Valentinians in the sixth book of the " Refutation." His system of Gnosticism is said to have been the most complicated of all; different sects and schools drew their systems from it; but that of Basilides, which Neander represents as having " the doctrines of emanation and dualism as the foundation of his system," is complicated enough, and fills one with amazement at its heaven-daring intrusion into the unrevealed mysteries of the divine nature and works.

* Professor Stokes, of Dublin University, in *Sunday at Home* (London).

The chief interest in Valentinianism for moderns is that it was very much like the popular fad of our day called Theosophy. Valentinus seems not to have considered paganism as necessarily wicked, but rather as a development preparatory to Christianity, and here we may see that the theory of Evolution applied to religion is, like Theosophy, no new thing under the sun.

It was against the teachings of this heretic and of Marcion that Polycarp made so emphatic a protest at the time of his visit to Anicetus in Rome.

Valentinus, like Basilides, quoted the New Testament, and, though he endeavored to read his system into it, recognized it as the standard of belief and the universally accepted authority among Christians. In this he was entirely unlike our modern Theosophists and religious Evolutionists.

But Hippolytus introduces us to another Gnostic, in whom we may rightly feel a very special interest; for, though he was drawn aside by the powerful current among the thinking men of his day of Gnosticism, and may be accused of holding a philosophy or science, "falsely so called," yet he showed great sincerity and earnestness. His chief claim, however, to our interest arises from the fact that not only did he, like Basilides and Valentinus, quote the New Testament as the inspired Word of God, but he wrote a commentary on it. He has the distinction of being the

first commentator on the New Testament so far
as is known.   This writer, Heracleon, was a Val-
entinian.   Heracleon's commentary is not now in
existence, unless, indeed, it be hidden away somewhere, as the " Refutation " was for so many ages
in the convent on Mount Athos.   But Origen has
preserved many extracts from it, and from these
we may learn how Heracleon regarded the New
Testament Scriptures.

On this point we have no inferior testimony.
Here is that of Canon Westcott:

" The introduction of the commentaries implies
the strongest belief in the authenticity and authority of the New Testament Scriptures ; and this belief becomes more important when we notice the
source from which they were derived.   They took
their rise among heretics, and not among Catholic Christians.   Just as the earliest fathers applied
to the Old Testament to bring out its real harmony
with the Gospel, so heretics endeavored to recon-
cile the Gospel with their own systems.   Commentaries were made where the want of them was
pressing.   *But, unless the Gospels had been generally accepted, the need of such works would not
have been felt.*

" Heracleon was forced to modify and turn
much that he found in St. John, which he would
not have done if the book had not been received
beyond all doubt.   And his evidence is more

valuable because it appears that he had studied the history of the apostles and spoke of their lives with certainty.

" The sense of the inspiration of the evangelists—of some providential guidance by which they were led to select each fact in their history and each word in their narrative—is not more complete in Origen.

" The first commentary on the New Testament exhibits the application of the same laws for its interpretation as were employed in the Old Testament. The slightest variation of language was held to be significant." *

This is exactly in accord with Dr. George Salmon's representation as to Heracleon's view of inspiration : " *His theory of inspiration is just the same as the one now popularly current in the church of Christ.*" †

Now it should be remembered that the value of the testimony of these heretics to the existence and acknowledged authority of the books of the New Testament is not at all dependent on the trustworthiness of the heretics as witnesses. The fact that they *appealed* to these books is evidence of their acceptance among Christians as the fountain of authority.

The existence of these writings from the days

---

* Westcott on the Canon, p. 304.
† See article of Professor Stokes in *Sunday at Home* (London).

of the apostles is indicated by another fact, which is perhaps not generally known. Both Basilides and Valentinus claimed a connection with apostles, each through a single link. Basilides claimed to have been instructed by one Glaucias, an interpreter of Peter, and Valentinus asserted that Theodas (or Theudas) was his instructor, and that this person was a disciple of Paul.

Now, whether these claims were true or false, the fact that they were *made* shows that these men lived early enough to have been thus connected with these apostles; for a claim which their contemporaries could not have believed would have prejudiced their cause instead of gaining acceptance for it. The learned Heracleon, for instance, could not have become a follower of Valentinus if the Theudas story had been incredible.

Basilides also claimed that secret discoveries were communicated to him by Matthias, the successor to the apostolate of Judas. He would hardly have made such a claim if it had been incredible to the men of his time.

Hippolytus begins with the Ophites, as if they were the first of these Gnostics, and indicates in book vi., chapter i., of the " Refutation " that they were the progenitors of the Basilidians and Valentinians. Their quoting the Gospel of John and other New Testament books as authorities, or

rather as *the authority*, with Christians indicates
that they were accepted among them from the
beginning.

Hippolytus (in book v.), treating of this heresy
at considerable length, notices some of the texts
which they misinterpreted to support their theories.
Among them are quotations from Matthew, Mark,
and Luke, besides such passages as these from
John's Gospel: i. 3, 4; ii. 1–11; iv. 10; vi. 44,
etc.; vi. 53.

How can the adherents of the Tübingen school
hold up their heads in the face of these facts?
How can they assert that these books were not
written until many years after the time in which
we find them extensively quoted? We would
consider it rather difficult to quote in this year
of our Lord 1896 from a book which is not to be
written till, say, 1926. But the Hegelian philosophy and German (or German*ized*) inner-consciousness can do wonderful things. If the facts
are against their theory they can readily conclude
that this makes it "so much the worse for the
facts." Common sense, however, would lead us
to look at the facts first and then hear the theories.

The Ophites (or Naasseni, as Hippolytus calls
them) existed as a sect before Christ. Says Mos-
heim: "This sect, which had its origin among the
Jews, was of a more ancient date than the Christian religion. A part of its followers embraced

the gospel, while the rest retained their primitive superstition; and hence arose the division of the Ophites into Christian and antichristian."

The fact that Hippolytus in dealing with the errors of this sect of Egyptian Jewish Gnostics represents them as quoting the New Testament books, is quite suggestive in view of the very early rise of this heresy.

Hippolytus also represents that Valentinus had his "starting-point" from Simon Magus and the philosophical systems of Plato and Pythagoras.* This may be true or it may not. But, whether the assertion is true or not, the fact that Hippolytus asserted it is indicative of the early rise of this heresy also, and the quotations which its advocates made from the New Testament *imply the existence of this collection of writings and their accepted authority among Christians from the apostolic age.*

The rise of the various phases of Gnosticism in connection with the spread of Christianity is a most interesting as well as a very saddening intellectual phenomenon. Egypt seems to have been a hotbed of these heresies. Alexandria was a center of wonderful intellectual activity. There met the advocates of the Egyptian and the Syrian *Gnosis* and the Greek philosophies.

As the Ophites originated in Egypt and both

* See " Refutation," book vi., chap. xv.

Basilides and Valentinus began to propagate their theories there, it seems probable that the assertion of Hippolytus about the " starting-point " of Valentinianism is true, in part at least.

There are certainly great differences and contrasts between these Gnostics and the school of Ferdinand Christian Baur. These early heretics received the New Testament writings as genuine and authoritative, while the advocates of the Tübingen theory endeavor to prove them to have been spurious documents, originating, with the exception of the Pauline epistles (the first four of which they acknowledge as genuine beyond all controversy, and others probably so), long after the apostolic age. Unlike the Tübingenists, who deny the supernatural, they not only acknowledged it, but each sect endeavored to show its various features as revealed in the Scriptures to be in full accord with the particular phase of philosophy held by itself.

In these and perhaps other respects there are great differences between the ancient advocates of the various forms of *Gnosis*, which gave them the name of Gnostics, and the modern advocates of " Reason," which gives them the name of Rationalists; but the ancient and the modern movements are precisely alike in one thing: they both embraced systems of philosophy and applied their principles to the facts and doctrines of Christianity.

As the result of the first great intellectual movement, we have Gnosticism in its Protean shapes, with its bythos and pleroma and demiurge and eons, and wild speculations about the unknown and the unknowable, in which we see men, as it were, vainly endeavoring and yet pretending to enter the very presence-chamber of God, for the purpose of revealing to the vulgar gaze those secrets of His own nature and work which He has not seen fit to reveal to mortal man; "intruding into those things which they have not seen, vainly puffed up by their fleshly mind."

As the result of the second movement, we find the Tübingenists taking as self-evident the conclusions of Hegel, and thus adopting as absolutely certain the main positions of a system characterized by the same idealistic pantheism as some, at least, of the Gnostics held, and, instead of trying to lay the Scriptures on the Procrustean bed·they have made, rejecting them altogether. Thus, while pursuing a course much like that of these heretics, they arrive at the conclusion of Agnosticism rather than that of Gnosticism; for it has long ago been recognized as the same thing to say "The universe [το παν] is God" and "There is no God." *Pantheism* is *atheism*.

XIII

FERDINAND CHRISTIAN BAUR

XIII

FERDINAND CHRISTIAN BAUR

Is it less amazing to look upon the course of Baur and his followers than on that of the Gnostics? Much instruction may be found in Baur's gradual progress from orthodoxy in early life to the extreme position which he afterward occupied as the founder of the Tübingen school of critics. It shows how the most powerful minds may be "spoiled through philosophy and vain deceit" when fully submitted to their influence.

The father of Ferdinand Christian Baur was a diligent and conscientious pastor, first in a little village near Stuttgart, and afterward at Blaubeuren, a small town at the southern base of the Swabian Alps. He was the teacher of his son until his fourteenth year, when he left home to attend school. In 1809 Ferdinand Christian Baur became a student of the University of Tübingen, where he was afterward to become so distinguished. His first production "was orthodox and supernaturalistic in its attitude." * Now for the influences that turned him.

Schleiermacher seems to have given the first touch that started this powerful and fertile intellect on its daring career of speculation in which, like an ignis fatuus, it has attracted and led astray so many of his own and the following generation. " The tendency and effect of Schleiermacher's exposition of the Christian faith are to reduce the supernatural to a minimum, and to make the little that remains appear as natural as possible, and so to satisfy the claims of science and philosophy, while endeavoring to do justice to the sentiments of believers." †

Then came Hegel. The Hegelian philosophy, adopted by Baur, was afterward applied by him to Christianity, and the result was the Tübingen theory of " tendencies."

Strauss, who had been a pupil of Baur, and whose work on the " Life of Jesus " has " overturned the faith of many," seems to have completed the work of destroying Baur's faith in the genuineness and inspiration of the New Testament.

A false philosophy is usually the fountain of a false theology. The early heretics adopted the various forms of heathen philosophy, as Hippolytus takes great pains to show, and the result

* Professor A. B. Bruce, in " Living Papers," vol. vii.
† *Ibid.*

in each case was some form of the fantastic mongrel monstrosity called Christian Gnosticism.

These modern critics have likewise adopted a philosophy and applied it to Christianity, and the result is not a mixture of the false system and Christianity, as in the first case, but a rejection of Christianity as a divine revelation and supernatural religion.

Under the powerful influence of his Hegelian philosophy, Baur tried to show that according to that philosophy there must be in the development of Christianity, as in the universe, a great process " which moves in a perpetual rhythm of affirmation, negation, and synthesis of opposites." *   In order to apply the Hegelian theory to the development of Christianity he made out that each book of the New Testament must have been the outcome of the " tendency " of thought at a particular period.   Hence, while he accepts the plain evidence for the genuineness of the first four epistles of Paul (Romans, 1 and 2 Corinthians, and Galatians), as, according to his theory, they suit the tendency of that period, he affirms that the Gospels could not have originated until much later, because his theory demanded it.   The tendency which he thinks must have given birth to the Gospels of Mark, Luke, and John could hardly have risen to high tide till about the middle of

---

* *Thesis, antithesis, synthesis.*

the second century, and hence these Gospels could not have been written till then. He holds that the Gospel of John comes after the time of affirmation and of negation and controversy, and represents the sentiment of those who were for the reconciliation of the two opposing schools he supposes to have arisen, and indicates the later tendency of "synthesis of opposites," so that the Gospel of John must have originated somewhere between 160 and 170 A.D.

Now when Hippolytus shows us that these sects, which began to arise certainly very soon after the death of John, if not before, quoted all the Gospels, and *his* more than any of the rest, we have before our eyes very plain evidence that, however ingenious the theory of Baur may have been and whatever may have been the quality of that genius which was able to draw so many minds in its train, Baur was entirely mistaken. The facts are too numerous, too plain, and from too many sources to admit of any doubt that the gospels were in existence many years before the dates which he gives them.

The conclusion of Zahn after the review of the evidence is that, "in view of the history of the text, opinions as to the origin of John's Gospel such as Baur has expressed must appear simply as madness. It follows, further, that the element which remains the same in all of the originals and of the versions [he had spoken of corruptions of the text] amid all the variations that crept into the text between 150 and 160 *must have been everywhere read at the beginning of the second century.*" Zahn concludes that the fourth Gospel, which Baur represents as not written till 160–170, was *everywhere read* in the year 100.

The argument from the "Refutation" of Hippolytus, who shows that it was quoted by Ophites, Valentinians, and Basilidians, leads without doubt to the same conclusion.

Thus the same conclusion is reached by two distinct paths as their common goal, and its validity is made the more evident by this fact. Zahn, looking at the text itself and studying its history in versions and variations, sees that the Gospel of John must have been in existence in the year 100; and we have seen our saint turning his search-light on these times and revealing the contentions of the various bands of Gnostics very soon after this date—contentions in which they made use of weapons taken from this armory, the Gospel of John. These weapons would have had no point or power if this Gospel had not been already generally known and accepted as authoritative.

Those were not the days of railroads, telegraphs, and steam printing-presses, and this general distribution and acceptance as authoritative of the fourth Gospel implies that *it had been written a considerable time before it was thus quoted* by opposing sects in different places. The slow multiplication of copies by the pen and the slow modes of travel in those times would make dissemination a slow process.

Not all of us are prepared to receive with full assurance the conclusions which are reached by mere critical processes. Many of us cannot feel entirely sure about the grounds of such conclusions; are uncertain about the " canons of criticism " employed; may fear, perhaps, that the mind of the critic may have been in some degree influenced by a priori preconceptions; or we may have to confess that, owing to ignorance or some mental defect on our part, we become a little confused by the talk about " uncials " and " cursives " and " palimpsests " and " groups " and " families " of texts and versions—that we grow a little dazed or dizzy as we are led along such highways of learned research, and a little uncertain about our footing on these heights of erudition, and somewhat faltering in the steps with which we proceed, if we proceed at all. But, without any " canons of criticism," or expert knowledge of texts, or any of the (to our apprehension) rather lumbering apparatus with which the professional critic sets out on his explorations, we can appreciate plain facts; and when our saint with his search-light shows us different sets of men in different countries quoting a certain book or set of books, we know, for one thing, that such writings are *in existence.* Otherwise they could not be *quoted.* And our plain, every-day common sense tells us that they *would* not be thus quoted unless they were of recognized authority on the matters under discussion, and that to have *acquired* such authority in different countries they must have been written a considerable time before the quotations were made.

The New Testament Scriptures were thus quoted soon after the close of the first century. *Therefore they must have been written before the close of that century.**

---

* For a fuller view of the career of Baur, the reader is referred to the admirable treatise, " Ferdinand Christian Baur and his Theory of the Origin of Christianity," by Professor A. B. Bruce, in " Living Papers," vol. vii., to which I am chiefly indebted for whatever of interest or value is to be found in this short sketch. —P. P. F.

XIV

ERNEST RENAN

XIV

ERNEST RENAN

To some it may have seemed unnecessary to
dwell at such length on the peculiar teachings of
Baur, whose theory has been so thoroughly re-
futed by facts that even those who hold the Hegelian philosophy see that it cannot be applied to
Christianity after Baur's manner.   Even Professor Harnack has admitted that, as the result of
recent discoveries, especially that of the " Diatessaron " of Tatian, " we learn . . . that about
160 A.D. our four Gospels had already taken a
place of prominence in the church and that no
others had done so; and that, in particular, the
fourth Gospel had taken a place alongside the
three synoptics." This acknowledgment, though
it lags far behind the natural interpretation of
the facts at which we have been looking and of
those to which we shall presently turn, thoroughly
overturns the conclusions of Baur.

But these facts are not generally known among

the great mass of readers, and the friends of Christianity should bestir themselves to make them known.

The Tübingen school is by no means dead, and, though the positions of its founder about the date of the Gospels have been shown to be false by facts which no one can honestly ignore, yet the skeptical principles of the leader are still animating a large number of followers, who, with some necessary change of view as to the origin of the Gospels, are yet cultivating in themselves and vast numbers under their influence the spirit of unbelief in Christianity as the divinely revealed and only true religion. The Hegelian philosophy is gaining a powerful and, it is to be feared, increasing influence * over cultivated minds. A notable article by one of the greatest thinkers of our times sounds a note of earnest warning against this most specious and yet most ensnaring of philosophical systems.†

In the words of another very able writer, " Of the many antichristian influences which have been at work in the minds of the more cultivated classes of men during the last fifty years, it is doubtful if any have had a more noxious and wide-spread effect than the works of this writer

* See *Contemporary Review* for February, 1895.
† See article in the *Presbyterian Quarterly* for January, 1895, by Dr. R. L. Dabney.

[Baur]. Not that his books, like those of Strauss or Renan, have ever commanded a wide circle of readers or appealed directly to the popular taste; but they have served as an armory whence popular writers have supplied themselves with weapons for their attacks upon the foundations of Christianity." *

Of this Hegelian tree, planted in Christian soil, we may think of Baur as the trunk, and Strauss and Renan as the main branches, and Harnack as a vigorous shoot from a Ritschlian bough.

Baur's works were not fitted to influence the reading public. They are to a great extent "caviare to the general." But they reached and powerfully influenced scholars who *could* reach the great mass of readers. If the root has been hidden from the vulgar eye, the branches to which it has supplied the sap have, unfortunately, attracted the gaze and gratified the appetite of the many who, like the Athenians and the sojourners in Athens, "spent their time in nothing else but either to tell or to hear some new thing."

Strauss influenced the more thoughtful class of readers, like George Eliot, who translated his "Leben Jesu," and received from it, doubtless, one of the chief influences which robbed her of her faith.

* Professor M. Maher, in the *Month* (London), November, 1892.

Renan has influenced that larger class who prefer the indulgence of fancy and the gratification of curiosity to real thinking, whose object in reading is enjoyment rather than finding the truth. He had a remarkable literary faculty which threw a charm over thoughts which, when weighed in the balance of sober reason, would be found utterly wanting. He was a born writer. When asked in childhood what he intended to do in life his answer was, " I will make books." His own account of his early dreams of ambition reminds one of De Quincey's account of the dreams of *his* childish imagination, stimulated by the beautiful and sublime in the architecture and services of the grand old church of his childhood. Renan, in the church of Tréguier, his birthplace, had dreams too. He tells us, in " Recollections of my Youth ": " During the services in church I used to fall into veritable reveries; my eye wandered in the vaulted roof; I read there I knew not what; I thought of the celebrity of the great men books tell of." His taste for literature was further cultivated and developed by an eloquent and energetic teacher, M. Dupanloup.

All his work in life shows the effect of this early bent and the influences about him. Accuracy and truth are made to yield to artistic excellence. He wrote what he felt would be pleasant to read and would secure the admiration of the reader for the author's genius. He wrote to please the many. He seems to have had the effect on the multitude always in view. " I have not existed completely, but for the public," is his own avowal.*

It is this that has made the skeptical principles of the Tübingen school so widely harmful. The skepticism of it, under a different form from that of the stricter adherents of Baur, yet the same in principle and influence, is brought within the reach of the general public by Renan. The poison is the same in both. In one case it is in the root, for the few who delve for it. In the other it is in the fruit, where it attracts the admiration and allures the appetite of the multitude.

His " Vie de Jésus " is like a romance. There is a charm in the sentences in which that wonderful life is described which leads captive the lover of the beautiful in literature, and the imagination finds a stimulus and gratification in the scenes and incidents of the Saviour's earthly career. Canaan, the land that flowed with milk and honey, rises before the mind's eye as another Eden, a very Paradise regained, as one follows the footsteps of the wonderful Galilean through His varied experiences.

Renan does not show a spirit of hostility, like the ordinary infidel, who exhibits his impiety in

* " Recollections."

every utterance. On the other hand, much of the time at least, he seems to invite us to admire Christ. He even speaks in a pious strain. In dedicating the book to his sister, who was with him in the Holy Land and assisting him, and who had died while he was lying unconscious under the power of the same disease which took her from his side, he says, " You were always persuaded that *the spirits truly religious* would be pleased with it." He seemed to have no doubt that he was one of " *the spirits truly religious.*"

Yet *the denial of the supernatural* in this wonderful life underlies all that he says of it, and the main purpose of the book is to eliminate it. But he emphasizes the natural and depicts it with the enthusiasm of the born artist.

In describing that Being whom angels adore and at whose feet the redeemed fall in the sweetest rapture of gratitude and love, he lavishes all the terms of florid rhetoric to exalt the beauty and attractiveness of His person, in order to conceal the blasphemous denial of His divinity—a blasphemy none the less wicked and harmful because clothed in such ornaments. It is the *more* dangerous on this account, because by thus pleasing the esthetic taste and eliciting the admiration of the reader for Christ as a man he the more easily satisfies him by making Him *such* a man, and thus robs Him of His crown as God over all. The thought-

less reader, dazzled by the brilliancy of the display, is not aware of his great loss, and, led by
the subtle charm along so pleasant and flowery a
path, is presently surprised to find himself in the
barren desert of unbelief, bereft of a Saviour, and
with all the sweet hope of a heaven in the future
faded from his soul.

But, while Renan represents Christ in a very
attractive light in some respects, it is not to be
inferred that he allows Him perfection. Especially in the latter part of His life he pretends to
find not only blunders, but instances of moral
dereliction. Thus Renan, who at one time invites
us to admire, if not to adore, at another bids us
find blemishes and criticise.

Thus this man, who seems so mild and gentle,
at last goes beyond most of the blatant infidels
in taking up the challenge of the Saviour, " Which
of you convinceth [R. V., " convicteth "] Me of
sin?"—a challenge which few have had the daring impiety to accept.

It is impossible to estimate the amount of evil
that has come to the readers of our time from
these sources. Thousands who never dream that
they are in danger as they bend over the strangely
fascinating novel or periodical, but, on the other
hand, feel very comfortably pious in finding themselves so deeply interested in religious reading,
are nevertheless imbibing a fatal virus. It is re-

ligious reading, but of the Renan sort. M. Doudan has described that very succinctly : "Renan donne aux hommes de sa génération ce qu'ils désirent en toutes choses—des bonbons qui sentent l'infini" ("Renan gives the men of his generation what they love in everything — sweetmeats scented with the infinite").* A religion without the obligation of holiness, without heaven or hell or Bible or God, but with only a delicate and undefined "scent of the infinite," has for many minds a strange fascination.

Poor dupes! The fascination is that of a serpent whose brilliant hues and graceful coil and facile speech are to rob them of the Eden of their faith by the promise of some higher "knowledge of good and evil." Alas! when their eyes are opened they will find themselves naked indeed, stripped of all that is best—"having no hope, and without God in the world."

There is a warning for us all in the story which Renan gives of the loss of his faith, though we cannot fully accept his account of it as in all parts correct. When he lays the blame on the architecture of the old church which he attended in childhood, we have to take this as one of the freaks of his lively fancy, and to think that this is one of the things which he wrote with a smile, and over against which, "if such things were

* Elmslie's essay on Ernest Renan, p. 45.

usual," he would have written "*cum grano.*"
We may well believe that his "dreams" in the
old cathedral might have developed his imagination; but it is hard to credit the assertion that
"the cathedral, a masterpiece of airy lightness,
a hopeless effort to realize in granite an impossible ideal, first of all warped my judgment. . . .
That architectural paradox made me a man of
chimeras."

Not the *architecture*, but the *teachings* of the
church were in a large degree responsible for his
moral and mental defects. Think of the effect
on an active mind of such a sham as he describes
a page or two further on, in his "Recollections
of my Youth":

"Upon the eve of the festival [of St. Yves]
the people assembled in the church, and on the
stroke of midnight the saint stretched out his arms
to bless the kneeling congregation. But if among
them all there was one doubting soul who raised
his eyes to see if the miracle really did take place,
the saint, taking just offense at such a suspicion,
did not move, and by the misconduct of this in-
credulous person no benediction was given."

Is it strange that a boy who was required to
believe in such transparent trickery as this should
soon cease to believe all that the tricksters taught
him? The miracles of Rome may deceive the
very dull and ignorant, but the effect of them on

most minds, where there is a capability for reasoning, is to make them skeptical about all religion because they see so plainly the fraud in this pretense.

But much of the fault was in Renan himself. From his own account, in both series of " Recollections," he seems to have been most thoroughly selfish, self-conscious, self-indulgent, almost wholly devoid of conscience or a sense of duty. Many shameless expressions, as well as his physiognomy, seem to indicate that he was not only an *intellectual* Sybarite, which he most certainly was, but a physical one too.

He jests lightly about the most serious matters, and the end in all he says seems to be never to lead to the truth or to benefit any soul, but simply to elicit admiration. He made himself his god, and it was easy for him to disbelieve in a Creator to whom he owed anything or a Judge to whom he would have to account for his life. That life must be to him an " enjoyment," and that seems to be his whole view of it. As he recognized no such thing as duty to God, it was natural that he should soon come to disbelieve in Him, and in His disregarded commands and revelation. Sin makes men blind to God and all that is of God. " If any man be *willing to do His will*, he shall *know*," etc. A willing and obedient heart is the organ of spiritual knowledge. It opens the soul's eyes wide to see and know the truth.

The utter incapability which Renan exhibits of being *serious* about anything is such a marked characteristic that some one has called him a man with a "cork soul." He seems incapable of staying below the surface in those dark depths and mysteries which he very often plunges into just to bound away from them and dance on the laughing waves of ironical raillery.

He speaks ironically and lightly on the most solemn themes, and jests about matters which it should sober every human being to think of. In the preface to his "Recollections and Letters" he says: "I confess I should not feel indifferent at being the object of a fine funeral in Paris. . . . And if they were to introduce in it a little feasting and revelry, oh, really, what harm would that do?"

He can write in the same light vein about the solemn mystery of the experiences of the soul after death:

"After my death, round the ruined Church of St. Michel, which frowns down on Tréguier, my soul shall nightly fly in the form of a white sea-mew, beating the bolted door and barred windows, seeking to enter the sanctuary, but ignorant of the secret way, wailing incessantly. ' 'Tis the soul of a priest that wants to say his mass,' the passing peasant will murmur. 'He will never find a clerk to make the responses,' another will answer. Just so. It is precisely this that has always been lacking in my church—the response," etc.

Well, he has now gone to those experiences about which his fancy could play so lightly. May we all be ready when called to try them!

The Hegelian philosophy doubtless had much to do with bringing Renan to that atheistic pantheism which took away all reverence and sense of duty, along with all solemnity, from his mind. And that philosophy is robbing many of their faith now, especially in our country and in Great Britain. Many of the most attractive teachers are instilling it into receptive and active minds among college and university students.*

But we have wandered long enough among the shadows, and it is time to come back to the light.

* It would be hard to find a better guide to the study of Renan than the essay referred to above, "Ernest Renan and his Criticism of Christ," by the Rev. W. G. Elmslie, M.A., "Living Papers," vol. iv. In connection with the "Recollections of my Youth," "Recollections and Letters," and "Life of Jesus," it has been freely used in preparing the foregoing sketch.

XV

THE SEARCH-LIGHT AND NEW DISCOVERIES
—THE "DIATESSARON"

XV

THE SEARCH-LIGHT AND NEW DISCOVERIES
—THE "DIATESSARON"

FOLLOWING the rays of the search-light, we now turn to two discoveries of very great interest—both of the present decade, and one of them very recent.

Among the characters to· whom Hippolytus calls our attention by no means the least interesting is Tatian.   Little is known of his personal history.   He was, as he himself tells us, an Assyrian, and a student of philosophy from his youth.   He was born about 110 A.D. and died in 172.

He was an earnest and conscientious seeker after truth.   After traveling in different countries in his extensive study of the philosophy of various schools, like Justin Martyr, he came to know the books of the Bible.   After studying these "barbaric books," as from the standpoint of his Greek culture he at first considered them, his conclusion was that the Old Testament Scriptures were "too old to be compared with the learning of the Greeks, too divine to be put on a level with their erroneous doctrines."

Irenæus tells us * that "he was a hearer of Justin's." Like his master, Justin Martyr, he did not cease to be a philosopher when he became a Christian, considering Christianity the very crown and capstone of philosophy.

Hippolytus classes him with the heretics, as did Irenæus before him. Many good men have been thus classed by other good men from whom they differed on some point of doctrine. He was an Encratite, or temperance man, and exalted the duty of self-control, especially in the denial of all fleshly appetites. That Oriental philosophy which was his birthright, the ground principle of which is the essential evil of matter and the goodness of spirit, was calculated to lead earnest minds into just such extreme views with regard to fasting and abstaining from marriage as are attributed to the Encratites.

Irenæus tells us that as long as Tatian had the companionship of Justin Martyr "he expressed no such views, but after his martyrdom he separated from the church," and also that he "composed his own peculiar type of doctrine." Among other things, "he declared that marriage was nothing but corruption and fornication." It seems, also, that he held the opinion that Adam was

* "Adv. Hæres.," book i., chap. xxviii.

never forgiven and saved, because the Scriptures represent that "in Adam all die." Before severely condemning him for this peculiar opinion about marriage we should remember that the doctrine of celibacy, as held by the Roman Catholics and other branches of nominal Christians in our own time, has this view of the marriage state as its unacknowledged, but not the less real, foundation.

But we are not interested now in Tatian's orthodoxy so much as in a deed which he did for the world—the production of a work which still exists, a work which in the early days of Christianity was in use in the Christian churches of Syria for a long time, and evidently, in translations, in other countries also; while its recent resurrection, as from a tomb where it had lain buried for many centuries, is a boon to our own times. It is probably the first harmony of the Gospels that was ever made.

Knowing the bearing which the existence of such a work prepared about 150 A.D. would have on the controversy about the origin of the Gospels, it was denied by some skeptical writers that any such book ever existed. In an able antichristian book, "Supernatural Religion," published in England in 1875, the anonymous author ventured to assert that "no one seems to have seen Tatian's harmony, probably for the simple reason that there was no such work."

The sarcasm would most certainly have been withheld if the author could have foreseen that St. Ephraem's "Commentary" on Tatian's "Diatessaron" would be published in May of the following year by Dr. Georgius Moesinger. In 1881 Zahn published his monograph, "in which, by means of citations from Ephraem's 'Commentary,' . . . he restored a considerable part of the original text of Tatian." *

This publication awakened interest in a MS. in the Vatican library which purported to be an Arabic translation of the "Diatessaron," and led Ciasca, an eminent Oriental scholar connected with the library, to examine it. He did not find time to translate and publish it immediately, and this delay seems to have been providentially directed, as many another disappointment and enforced delay has been, for the best result in the end.

While waiting for an opportunity to do the work Ciasca one day showed the codex to the apostolic vicar-general of the Catholic Copts in Egypt, who happened to be in the library. As soon as he looked into it he said that there was another copy of the work in the possession of a gentleman in Egypt, and that he could have it brought to Rome. He succeeded in doing so,

* Article in the London *Month*, December, 1892, by M. Maher.

and the following is a description of the Egyptian codex:

"The codex consists of three hundred and fifty-three leaves. There is no date attached, but the MS. seems to belong at the latest to the fourteenth century. The pages are nine by six and one quarter inches, inclosed in an illuminated square of golden, red, and purple lines, with an ornamentation of golden asterisks." *

This second MS. was of very great use, as it supplied lacunæ and cleared up obscure readings in the first.

The first MS. was called the Vatican and the second the Borgian, as it was deposited in the Borgian library.

Now, in a new edition in 1879, the author of "Supernatural Religion" ventured to say, "It is obvious that there is no evidence of any value connecting Tatian's Gospel with those in our canon." †

Two years later Zahn's reproduction of a part of Tatian's text appeared; four years later Ciasca published his description of the codex, containing the text itself, and in 1888 he had his long-delayed translation (into Latin), with the Arabic

* Article in the London *Month*, December, 1892, by M. Maher.

† Vol. ii., p. 157, 1879. Quoted by Dr. Wace in his tract on "The Authenticity of the Four Gospels."

text, issued from the press of the Propaganda in time to present it to the pope on the occasion of his jubilee.

These were notable collisions of false assertions with facts which served to demonstrate their falsity and proclaim it, as it were, from the very housetops.

Many questions crowd for answer here. What is the date of this work? Are the Gospels of the " Diatessaron " " our Gospels " only, or are there mingled with them parts of apocryphal Gospels? Does Tatian seem to regard these writings of merely historical interest, or as the record of a divine revelation? Are the Gospels quoted placed in separate columns, or are they interwoven so as to make a continuous narrative?

In the endeavor to answer these questions I shall rely chiefly on the account given by Professor Maher, of Stonyhurst, from whose interesting articles in the *Month* I have already quoted.

As to the date of Tatian's work entire certainty cannot be attained. There are indications, however, that it does not belong to the latter part of his life—the Encratite period. These are found in the fact that he does not omit or modify anything which would be hostile to his later views on marriage. For instance, he gives in full the account of the marriage in Cana of Galilee.

The " Diatessaron " is conjecturally dated at

A.D. 150. It contains our four Gospels, without a trace of any of the later apocryphal Gospels. One or two expressions occur which are not to be found in our "received" text, nor in that of Westcott and Hort, the text chiefly used in preparing the Revised Version, but they have been traced to the Curetonian Syriac text, and of the significance of this we will presently catch a glimpse.

The Gospels do not appear in separate columns, but are interwoven so as to form a continuous narrative.

Tatian's treatment of these Gospels plainly shows that he regards them as part of the inspired Word of God. The "chaff" of which Cardinal Gibbons speaks had evidently not yet become mingled with the wheat, so as to make it necessary for a church council to assemble and go to sifting. Ecclesiasticism was the great cultivator of this fictitious "chaff," as any one will see who will take the Ignatian epistles, for instance, with the shorter and longer recensions in parallel columns. The interpolations which make a large part of the longer recension are hierarchical and ecclesiastical "chaff" indeed.

Tatian's Gospels are our four, and the very name of his work emphasizes it. It is "The Dia Tessaron"—"The Through Four": the one life through the four evangelists.

Now, as to the text which Tatian must have used, Professor Maher remarks: " A writer as familiar as Tatian certainly was with all the literature of his time, and personally acquainted with St. Justin and the leading Christian churches, . . . would have been certain to have provided himself with the best and oldest MSS. within his reach. This fact should never be forgotten in estimating the value of the ' Diatessaron.' "

Let us remember in forming this estimate such facts as these: Tatian was associated with Justin Martyr, a man of learning and eminence, who spoke with great freedom to Roman emperors, as his two " Apologies " show; and he must have known many Christians who, when John's Gospel was written, were of age and could well remember its first reception among the Christian churches. Could this accomplished scholar, born ten or twelve years after John's death, with such advantages as he had for gaining information, and with so critical a turn of mind, have made the mistake of receiving a spurious document as a Gospel written by the beloved disciple?

Notice the way in which he uses both this and the synoptic Gospels. The first words of the " Diatessaron " are those with which the Gospel of John begins: " In the beginning was the Word, and the Word was with God, and the Word was God." Professor Maher tells us, " The greatest

care is displayed to adhere as far as possible to
the very words of the several evangelists, and
brief texts and fragments of texts are industri-
ously pieced together, so that an elaborate mosaic
is the result." On this Professor Maher remarks:
"If Tatian or any other author of his time had
merely written that 'the four Gospels are universally believed to be inspired,' it would still be
possible to dispute as to what he meant by the
word 'inspired.' But the 'Diatessaron' provides
us with an object-lesson which makes the matter
plain. The reverent care and labor with which
the texts of the four evangelists are interwoven,
and their sentences and phrases preserved, proves
the belief in the peculiar sacredness, in the mysterious virtue in their briefest utterances. . . .

"It is only the conviction of *the divine character of the Gospels*, both on the part of the author
and his readers, which could have given rise to
the attempt at such a harmony."

This last sentence embodies what must be the
conclusion of every thoughtful and unprejudiced
mind. What Canon Westcott says of the appearance, at nearly the same time in which the "Diatessaron" was prepared, of the "Commentary"
of Heracleon is entirely applicable here: "Unless
the Gospels had been generally accepted, the need
of such works would not have been felt." We
may further say that, unless these Gospels had

been not only accepted, but were very highly
prized and venerated, and generally and carefully
studied by Christians, it is hardly probable that
such a work as the "Diatessaron" of Tatian
would have been prepared and placed at their
service. It would certainly never have been done
with the evidences of such reverential care if, as
some of our friends would have us believe, at this
time everything was in a state of uncertainty
about the sacred records, and there was doubt
as to what was wheat and what was "chaff." In
the clear light and winnowing wind of these discoveries, much that has heretofore masqueraded
as "impartial criticism" has been found to be
very aptly designated by the last word of the last
sentence, and forever whirled away from the field
of controversy. With all the fine phrases of its
vaunted erudition, it is shown to be but "chaff"
indeed.

Tatian, as we have seen, had as his instructor
in righteousness no less a person than Justin
Martyr.

Justin, in writing his "Apologies" to heathen
emperors, very naturally did not give the names
of the evangelists in quoting from them, as this
would have added nothing to the weight of what
was written with these men. But, in spite of the
fact that he was writing to heathen men who
were probably ignorant of the writers of the New

Testament, it is remarkable that his arguments are full of quotations from and plain references to these writings. It has been remarked that, if all other sources of information were destroyed, we could learn the main facts of our Saviour's life through the quotations of Justin Martyr alone. I think the statement could be made still stronger. From chapters xxx.–lx. of the first " Apology " alone we could learn all the cardinal facts of our Saviour's life and work. Though, philosopher as he was, he reasoned in the manner of the philosophers of his day, it is wonderful to see his reasonings saturated with scriptural thought and plentifully intermingled with quotations from the Old and New Testaments.

The fact that his pupil, Tatian, arranged the four Gospels into a harmony makes it clearer and more indisputable that the four Gospels were already gathered together and fully recognized as the authentic and inspired memorials of the life of Christ, and that the quotations and references of Justin Martyr are not a record of mere verbal traditions handed down among the Christians. That these "memoirs" were already not only gathered, but in constant use in Christian worship, is made perfectly clear by Justin's own words: " On the day which is called Sunday there is an assembly in one place of all who dwell either in towns or in the country, and the memoirs of the apostles or the writings of the prophets are read as long as the time permits." *

That these "memoirs of the apostles" were our four Gospels was quite plain before the discovery of Tatian's " Diatessaron," for, as Professor Gildersleeve remarks: " As Irenæus, Clement, and Tertullian quote our Gospels, the negative theory requires us to believe that in the short interval an entire change of Gospels was made throughout all the different and distant provinces of the Roman empire at a time when concerted action through general councils was unknown, and that, too, in so silent a manner that no record of it remains in the history of the church."

Since the discovery of Tatian's harmony, doubt is no longer possible, for there we find our four Gospels interwoven by Justin's pupil, Tatian, so as to form a continuous account of our Saviour's words and deeds.

Let us now turn to a still more recent and exceedingly interesting discovery. We shall find it another of that cloud of witnesses God, in His providence, is raising from the dust, in these latter days of doubt and skepticism, to attest the genuineness of the New Testament Scriptures.

* First " Apology," chap. lxvii.

XVI
"THE NEW SYRIAC GOSPELS"

XVI

"THE NEW SYRIAC GOSPELS"

IN the *Contemporary Review* for November, 1894, there appeared a most interesting article by Professor J. Rendel Harris, the eminent textual critic, in which he described a palimpsest recently discovered in the St. Catharine Convent, on Mount Sinai.

Some readers may need to be informed that a palimpsest is a manuscript in which the original writing has been partially erased by the use of pumice-stone or some other means, and written over with some later production. The expensiveness of parchment led to the frequent use of old manuscripts for later writings in this way.

The place had already been made famous by the discovery there, in 1859, of the Sinaitic Codex, by Tischendorf, and the discovery in 1890, by Professor J. Rendel Harris, of the long-lost "Apology" of Aristides.

An interesting fact about the discovery of " The

New Syriac Gospels," * of which Professor Harris gives an account in the *Contemporary*, is that it was made by a woman.

In the spring of 1892 Mrs. Agnes Smith Lewis, the widow of the Rev. S. S. Lewis, the librarian of Corpus Christi College, of Cambridge University, England, in company with her twin sister, Mrs. Gibson, also of Cambridge, made a journey to the East, and, induced by their interest in Professor J. Rendel Harris's then recent discovery of the "Apology" of Aristides in the library of the Convent of St. Catharine, they went there.

In the words of Mrs. Lewis, "Among the Syriac books which they [the monks] showed us, I soon picked up a volume of one hundred and seventy-eight leaves, nearly all glued together with some greasy substance. I separated them, partly with my fingers and partly with the steam of a kettle. They had the more fascination for me that no human eye had, evidently, looked on them for centuries; and I soon perceived that it was a palimpsest, whose upper, or later, writ-

* For a fuller account the reader is referred to "The Four Gospels in Syriac," translated from the Sinaitic palimpsest by the late Robert L. Bensley . . . and by J. Rendel Harris, M.A., lecturer of the University of Cambridge, etc. (Macmillan), and to "How the Codex was Found," by Mrs. Gibson, and to "Translation of the Four Gospels from the Syriac," by Mrs. A. S. Lewis, the discoverer (Macmillan).

ing contained the stories of woman saints, while
the under one was the four Gospels."

She determined to photograph the whole palimpsest, which she did, with the assistance of
Mrs. Gibson. Great difficulties had to be over-
come in order to accomplish this undertaking,
but the work was at last completed, and the sisters returned to England with their prize. These
Syriac Gospels were found to have much in common with those discovered by Cureton, and which
bear his name. The colophon of the MS. also
indicates its connection with the Curetonian Syriac MS.

Partly owing to the spoiling of some of the
photographs in developing, it became necessary,
in order to obtain a fully satisfactory result, that
another visit should be made to Mount Sinai. The
sisters returned to the convent, in company with
Professor Harris and Professors Bensley and Bur-
kitt, and their wives, and they together worked
" from sunrise to sunset " for more than a month.
A "chemical reviver" was used, and thereby the
old codex, " looking out of its palimpsest prison
through the bars of a later writing," was brought
more fully into the light.

The author of " Parchments of the Faith " closes
his account, written in 1894, by saying : " Unfortunately for these pages, the publication of the full
results of the study of the document is delayed."

The want thus referred to has been supplied by the article of Professor Harris in the *Contemporary*. He tells us that he and his assistants " have been able to restore from the actual MS., with the assistance of Mrs. Lewis's photographs, the greater part of the four Gospels from the faded writing in which they appear; and this we have done, often for whole pages without the loss of a word or a letter. . . . We have, therefore, a transcript of the four Gospels in Syriac, dating from a very early period, say the fifth century, and representing not unfaithfully *a translation which must have been made far back in the second century.* Examination shows that it is closely connected with the Syriac version which was edited by Cureton in 1859, and which is called after his name. There is not the least doubt that, as far as Syriac Gospels are concerned, a text has been recovered superior in antiquity to anything yet known, and one that often agrees with all that is most ancient in Greek MSS.; a text which the advanced critics will at once acknowledge to be, after allowance has been made for a few serious blemishes, superior in purity to all extant copies, with a very few exceptions; and at the same time a text which by its dogmatic tendencies will arrest the interest of theologians of every school of thought."

We are naturally anxious to know the nature

of a set of "blemishes" in a text of the New Testament which Professor Harris considers so old and, in general, unusually true to what the best MS. authorities attest as the original text.

It has been said that, though a vast number of changes were made in producing the Revised Version of the English Bible, not a single doctrine is at all affected by the revision. This cannot be said of the text which was discovered by Mrs. Lewis. Should that be followed, belief in the cardinal fact of Christianity—the incarnation of Christ, our Lord—would be overthrown. It is evidently the design of this copy of the Gospels to do this. In the words of Professor Harris: "But the most original feature in our MS., and perhaps the most archaic of its peculiarities, is the suggestion on its very first page of another version of the birth of our Lord, by readings which definitely and designedly assign to Joseph, the husband of Mary, the paternity of Jesus."

I need not dwell on this, except to say that the theory of a *mistake* as the explanation of the introduction of these changes into the first chapter of Matthew is untenable. The changes are introduced too systematically to admit of any such explanation. They are such as these: Verse 16: "*Joseph* [to whom was espoused the Virgin Mary] *begat Jesus*, who is called Christ." Verse 21: "*She shall bear thee* a son," etc. Verse 25:

"*And she bare him a son*, and he called His name Jesus."

Professor Harris reminds us of the formula, "When the cause of a variant is known the variant itself will disappear." The cause of the variant here is very clearly seen. It is the settled purpose to discredit the miraculous birth by which Christ became incarnate. As Professor Harris says, it is evident that "an enemy hath done this." Who is that enemy?

Here our saint with his search-light comes to our aid. In the "Refutation of all Heresies," book vii., chapter xxi., we have the following:

"But a certain Cerinthus, himself being disciplined in the teaching of the Egyptians, asserted that the world was not made by the principal Deity, but by some virtue that was an offshoot from that Power which is above all things, and which yet is ignorant of the God that is above all.

"And he supposed that *Jesus was not generated from a virgin*, but that He was *born son of Joseph and Mary, just in a manner similar to the rest of men;* and that [Jesus] was more just and more wise [than all the human race].

"And [Cerinthus alleges] that, after the baptism [of our Lord], Christ, in the form of a dove, came down upon Him from that absolute sovereignty which is above all things."

Thus we find Cerinthian adoptionism endeavoring to drive the doctrine of the divine conception and incarnation of Christ from the Scriptures by corrupting the text.

While we shudder at the horrible wickedness of such speculations about a matter which has been revealed in the Scriptures, we have one reason to be thankful that this text of the Gospels has come to light. Setting aside this variant in the " nativity " passages, the text is an excellent one, and very old. This heresy that has stamped its cloven foot upon it has, in doing so, helped to fix the date of its origin. Says Professor Harris, " It need not be the very Gospel used in Cerinthian circles, but it is certainly sufficiently like to it to share with the Gospel spoken of by Epiphanius in a common designation." Epiphanius, as well as Irenæus and our own Hippolytus, besides others, tells us of this heresy of Cerinthus. And *Cerinthus was a contemporary of the Apostle John.* The tradition that John turned his back upon him in Ephesus, in horror at his impious doctrines, may or may not be true; but there is nothing improbable in it.

The gentle John became a very Boanerges, even in his old age, when some began to deny that " Jesus Christ had come in the flesh." The heresy of Docetism is supposed to be referred to. But is not Cerinthianism a twin brother to that? Cerinthus held that Christ only abode with the man Jesus for a time, and deserted Him at the time of the crucifixion. Thus Cerinthus endeavors, like many in our own times, to eliminate from Christianity that which is its central fact, the atoning death of our Redeemer, the efficacy of which depends on the fact which even the heathen centurion who had charge of the crucifixion was constrained to acknowledge in the words, " Surely this was the Son of God."

It seems plain that a version bearing a distinct Cerinthian character must have been made at the time when the Cerinthian heresy was propagated, as it was evidently intended to be an instrument for its propagation.

Such marks may very generally be relied on in settling the date of a document. They bear an analogy to the geological record, the " testimony of the rocks," in the undesigned and imperishable character of such a record; but they are much less liable to misinterpretation. We may take an illustration from times much nearer our own, and be able to see more clearly how dates are fixed in this way.

Suppose that, some hundreds or thousands of years hence, there should be found, among Christians as ignorant of our English tongue as we are of the Syriac of the second century, a copy of an English Bible in which eminent scholars among them, who should understand this old language (as some among us now know the Syriac), had observed some remarkable peculiarities which clearly differentiated it from other English versions with which they were acquainted—such peculiarities, for instance, as these:

Acts xiv. 23: " Ordained to them *priests* in every church." 1 Timothy v. 17: "Let the *priests* that rule well be esteemed worthy of double honor." Titus i. 5: " And shouldest ordain *priests* in every city." James v. 14: " Is any man sick among you? let him bring in the *priests* of the church," etc. And then such as these: Matthew iii. 1, 2: " And in those days cometh John the Baptist, preaching in the desert of Judea, and saying, DO PENANCE: for the kingdom of heaven," etc. Mark vi. 12: " And going forth, they preached that men should *do penance.*" Luke xiii. 3: " But, unless you shall *do penance,* you shall all likewise perish." Luke xvi. 30: " No, father Abraham: but if one went unto them from the dead, they will *do penance,*" etc.

Such scholars would naturally ask, " How is it that the word ' elder,' or ' presbyter,' found in other English versions, the equivalent of the Greek *presbuteros*, is here replaced by this word ' priest,' which in English designates the men who offered sacrifices under the Jewish law, or ministered at heathen altars, the equivalent of which in Greek is *hiereus?* And what process is this which is put under the name of 'doing penance,' and which is made essential for the pardon of sin and escape from 'perishing'?"

Then if these scholars, instead of beginning to theorize, should go to investigating facts, and should turn the search-light of history on the British Isles, where English is the common tongue, and on the continent of Europe, they would find that in the sixteenth century a great movement, called the Reformation, took place. They would find that this Reformation was accomplished chiefly by giving the Bible to the people in their own language, and that when the waves of the great movement began to agitate England there was felt a great want. The people must have that Bible which had so roused the Germans. Then came a period of Bible translation. God raised up a wonderful man, William Tyndale, to give the Bible to the English people. Other English translations were made with various special aims, of which their pages bear evident traces; but, whatever patterns may have been wrought into the fabric, Tyndale's constituted the warp and woof of them all.

Church and state in England were arrayed against the movement. Many lives were sacrificed, Tyndale's among the rest. But the people would have the Word of God, in spite of stake and gibbet.

The search-light of history would reveal a rapid progress of the Reformation through the circulation of the Scriptures, so that the majority of the nation became its advocates.

These investigators would naturally inquire, "Why was a reformation needed, and what brought about that state of things which called so loudly for it?" "Who took away this Bible for which there is now such a demand on the part of the people?"

As they turn the search-light back upon the earlier centuries, they find that this state of things was brought about chiefly by the ministers of the gospel being replaced by *priests*, who, instead of pointing to the great sacrifice of Calvary, turned the Lord's Supper into a sacrifice, and bade those whom they would allow to partake of it believe in it as the very body and blood of Christ.

Then it would be found that these priests gained more and more ghostly power, and formed themselves into ranks and orders, till at last one of them was placed on a throne, and kings and emperors were made his servants.

Then the question would arise, "How did these priests accomplish this wonderful feat?" The search-light of history would reveal the answer. It would show these men pretending to stand between men and their God, and to be able to forgive their sins. It would dart its rays into thousands of dark cuddies called confessionals, and would show in each a priest sitting, while a penitent man or woman or child knelt and told to the priest the innermost secrets of heart and life. Then the priest would be seen prescribing a " penance " for each penitent, and, whether doing the penance involved self-torture, or the resigning of possessions to the church and going to a convent or monastery, the priest found the requirement, " Do penance or perish," a powerful instrument in his hands, and by it brought down king and peasant.

Now, when the Reformation began in England, and the English Bible made plain the way of salvation through Christ alone, the " one Mediator " between God and man, vast multitudes turned away from the priests and confessionals, and, instead of " doing penance," repented of their sins, and believed on the Lord Jesus Christ, that they might be saved.

Now our investigators would find that the period of English Bible translation, in connection with this great movement, the Reformation, began with the publication of Tyndale's translation of the New Testament in 1526, and of the whole Bible in 1535, and ended with the publication of King James's version in 1611.

They might never have turned their search-

light on Rheims or Douay; yet, from the peculiarities of the version which had in it the " priest "
and " do penance " features, they would have no
hesitation in saying, " A priest hath done this."
They would feel sure, too, that it was done during this period of English Bible translation ex-
tending from 1526 to 1611. Having found that
it had been for centuries the policy of the priests
to keep the Bible from the people, and that for
this purpose they had kept it locked up in a dead
language, they would see that when they now
translated it into the English language they did
it because they felt obliged to change their policy
to some extent, though not the principle underly-
ing it. Circumstances forced them to do it. By
the translation of the Bible into English the light
had been turned on, and the people as they read
began to find the scales falling from their eyes.
They saw that in the New Testament there was
nothing about priests and penances in the Christian church. The priests and sacrifices belonged
to the preparatory dispensation of those types and
shadows which pointed to Christ, the great High
Priest, who should offer for our redemption the
sacrifice of Himself. " So Christ was *once* offered
to bear the sins of many " (Heb. ix. 28). " For by
one offering He hath perfected forever them that
are sanctified." The people were rapidly learning
this great truth, and were turning away from the

altars where pretended priests were offering an endless succession of pretended propitiatory sacrifices of the mass.

What shall the priests do? They make a desperate resolve. If these things are not in the Bible *they will put them there.* Hence comes the " priest " and " penance " version of Rheims and Douay.

It was an artful scheme to use the very sledgehammer that had broken the bars of the people's prison for forging their fetters anew. If they *must* know of the Bible from English translations, they shall have one that shall teach them of priests and penances. " For by this craft we have our wealth."

Thus the Douay version, if in a future age it should be found without colophon and date, could easily be identified and dated by the finger-marks of the priests. The close of the sixteenth or the beginning of the seventeenth century would be set down as its birth-hour.

Just so the new codex of the Syriac Gospels discovered by Mrs. Lewis at Mount Sinai is marked, by the footprints of Cerinthianism in it, as belonging to the period of this heresy.

The connection traced by Professor Harris between the new Syriac Gospels and the Curetonian Syriac text gives another indication of the very early origin of the text of the former. This

connection is of such a kind as to indicate quite
clearly the superior antiquity of the newly discovered text.

The Curetonian emphasizes the virginity of
Mary by changes in the very text which Cerinthus or his followers changed in the endeavor to
make the "nativity" passages teach, not the supernatural incarnation of Christ, but the natural
birth, by ordinary generation, of Jesus. The
changes are such as these: In Matthew i. 25, instead of "took his *wife*," the Curetonian has
"took *Mary*." In i. 20, the words of the angel,
"fear not to take to thee Mary *thy wife*," are
changed to "fear not to take to thee Mary *thine
espoused*." In i. 19, "Joseph, *her husband*," appears simply as "*Joseph*."

Hence it seems clear, as Professor Harris tells
us, that the Curetonian text is the result, as to
this feature, of an endeavor to correct the Cerinthian error.

Of course the text on which corrections are
made must be older than the corrections. *A
document must be older than a corrected edition of
itself.* It seems almost certain, then, that the
text of the Gospels discovered at Mount Sinai is
one of which the Curetonian is a correction;
therefore it must be older than the Curetonian.
As the "Diatessaron" of Tatian shows, according to Professor Harris, a connection with the

Curetonian, the inference is that it, too, is more recent than the newly discovered Cerinthian text. This makes it look as if the latter was the text used in Cerinthian circles.

Now this Cerinthian text was a corruption of an original, doctored in the " nativity " passages to sustain the adoptionist theory. This text in which the changes in these passages were made must, of course, have been older than the corrupted Cerinthian text. The passages changed make the text in these places inconsistent with itself in other places, and thus point to an older, self-consistent, unmutilated text.

We find, then, in these newly discovered Gospels, another indication of the existence of this part, at least, of the New Testament within the first century.

Our quest is well-nigh ended. There has been no effort to present the whole body of evidence of the genuineness of the New Testament Scriptures. We have only traveled through the obscure ways of this comparatively little-known age by the help of our saint's search-light.

We have found, even by an examination of the ground on which this light falls, clear and cumulative evidence that the New Testament came down from apostolic times, and that from the first it was received as the authority to which all parties appealed.

Our first excursion for research was along the path of Hippolytus's spiritual ancestry, and we found Irenæus, his teacher, quoting in his extant works every book of the New Testament, with the exception of two very brief epistles, while Polycarp, the teacher of Irenæus, in the only writing of his which is extant, quotes the New Testament so extensively that the letter is a mosaic made up, in large part, of gems from the New Testament writings. And Polycarp was contemporary with the Apostle John for almost forty years. This of itself would be sufficient; but we find corroborative testimony.

Our second excursion was by the way of the Gnostic heresies to which Hippolytus introduces us, and we found Valentinus and Basilides (the latter a younger contemporary of John) quoting the New Testament writings and appealing to them as the recognized authority in religious discussion, while we found Heracleon, a disciple of Valentinus, actually writing a commentary in which he shows a strict view of the inspiration of the New Testament.

Our third inquiry was concerning Tatian, of whom Hippolytus speaks, and in his newly discovered "Diatessaron" we found a harmony of the four Gospels in which the most punctilious regard was paid to the very words and phrases of the evangelists, as Tatian interweaves them into a continuous narrative. This indicates that these Gospels had long been accepted as the genuine " memoirs of the apostles " concerning the Lord Jesus, of which Justin Martyr tells the Emperor Antoninus Pius that they were used in Christian worship along with the Old Testament Scriptures.

And at last, guided by our saint's light, we found Cerinthus, a contemporary of John, teaching that our Lord was born of human parents, by ordinary generation, and lo! there rises from its tomb on Mount Sinai a codex of the four Gospels with the footprints of this heresy in it.

Thus we find these four roads converging to a point within the apostolic age. As we approach it, first from one direction and then from another, we behold, rising in the distance there, that sublime structure from which has shone through the ages a celestial light, and from whose threshold flows a life-giving stream—the finished temple of divine revelation.

XVII

THE NEW TESTAMENT IN THE FIRST CENTURY

197

XVII

THE NEW TESTAMENT IN THE FIRST CENTURY

NO one acquainted with the subject will contend that the books of the New Testament were gathered together into a volume by supernatural means as soon as they were written, and that as soon as the last word was indited every church was found in possession of a completed New Testament. While the New Testament writings are, as we verily believe, of supernatural origin and character, " inspired,"—God-breathed (*Theopneustai*), —they were produced through natural agencies, were called forth, as some of the epistles especially show, by certain exigencies, and bear the mark of the natural powers, tastes, and culture of their authors. The *distribution* of them was doubtless by natural means too, and undoubtedly some churches received some of them before other churches. The multiplication of copies was accomplished by the slow and tedious process of writing and was far from instantaneous. Dr. B. B. Warfield, in the *Presbyterian Quarterly*, April, 1895, well describes the process as follows:

" The Bible was circulated only in hand copies slowly and painfully made, and an incomplete copy, obtained, say, at Ephesus in A.D. 68, would be likely to remain for many years the Bible of the church to which it was conveyed, and might, indeed, become the parent of other copies, incomplete like itself, and thus the means of providing a whole district with incomplete Bibles. Thus, when we inquire after the history of the New Testament canon, we need to distinguish such questions as these: 1. When was the New Testament canon completed? 2. When did any one church acquire a completed canon? 3. When did the completed canon, the complete Bible, obtain universal circulation and acceptance? 4. On what ground and evidence did the churches with incomplete Bibles accept the remaining books when they were made known to them?" He answers the first question thus: " The canon of the New Testament was completed when the last authoritative book was given to any church by the apostles." His conclusion on the whole matter is: " But from the time of Irenæus down, the church at large had the whole canon as we now possess it."

Pursuing the four ways made plain by the search-light of our saint, we have at each approach to the apostolic age found the New Testament already in existence. We have looked, as it were, from four standpoints on the verge of the first century, and each time we have caught a glimpse of this divinely erected edifice. Have we been mistaken? Was it a mere mirage, a reflection back into the first century of what only grew to its completion late in the second?

Whether what we have seen is a mirage or a reality will be best determined by a close approach and a careful examination. This examination we must make for ourselves, as the results have so important a personal interest for us and a mistake would be so disastrous; but in making the approach we need not disdain such assistance as that of Renan and Baur, men who have carefully examined this region and who should be competent guides for this purpose, *so far as the possession of the requisite information goes.*

Renan says of the four epistles of Paul which occur first in our New Testament, those to the Romans, the Corinthians, and the Galatians, that they are " incontestables et incontestées " (" indisputable and undisputed "), and also that " les critiques les plus sévères, tels que Christien Baur, les acceptent sans objection " (" the most exacting critics, such as Christian Baur, accept them without objection ").*

As these four epistles are admitted by the most

* " St. Paul," pp. v., vi. Quoted by Dr. Wace in " Evidential Conclusions from the Four Greater Epistles of Paul," pp. 3, 4.

advanced critics as the writings of the Apostle Paul, we need not discuss their authenticity. Taking our stand, then, in this part of the New Testament, we may at least begin our examination of this part of what Christians hold to be the completion of God's revelation.

What must strike any one as remarkable about these four epistles is that they proceed upon a certain set of facts, that these facts are many of them altogether out of the mere natural order, and that they all cluster about a PERSON who is entirely unlike any historical character. We find the acknowledged writer of these four epistles showing every conceivable sign of the utmost sincerity as he unfolds these facts, and deduces certain doctrines from them, and lays down certain rules of practical conduct for those to whom he is writing, while he evidently accepts these doctrines and rules as the norm of his own thinking and living.

Now, as we look further into the New Testament, we see that these facts which Paul presupposes and builds upon in these epistles are given in detail in four other books called "Gospels," written by Matthew, Mark, Luke, and John, and chiefly by the first three of these. The very natural presumption is that these Gospels, or some of them at least, had been written when Paul wrote these epistles *which are acknowledged to be*

his. It is not claimed at all that this conclusion
is absolutely necessary, but it is certainly reasonable and probable. The use which Paul makes
of these facts concerning Christ implies that he
had definite and full information about them, and
we find such information in these Gospels.

It seems clear, then, that as these facts about
Christ underlie all the teaching of these epistles,
and as the system called Christianity (*which is
absolutely unique*) is precisely the same as presented in these epistles and in the life, death,
resurrection, ascension, and teachings of Christ
recorded in these Gospels, it is incredible that the
Gospels could have originated in a later age, as
the Tübingen school contended.

Here we can again allow M. Renan to take us
by the hand and lead us into these rooms which
we have been viewing from other apartments,
though we protest in advance against any conclusions he might wish us to adopt as to what
we see in them. We prefer to see and conclude
for ourselves. We will take his hand, but keep
our eyes. Renan acknowledges that the Gospel
of Luke is in all probability genuine. He says:
" As to Luke, doubt is scarcely possible. . . .
The author of this Gospel is certainly the same as
the author of the Acts of the Apostles. Now the
author of the Acts seems to be a companion of
St. Paul, a character which accords completely

with St. Luke."* He concludes: "We think, therefore, that the author of the third Gospel and of the Acts is in all reality Luke, the disciple of Paul."

Baur, by his doctrine of "tendencies," tried to make the world believe that our Gospels represent the stages of religious discussion of the first and second centuries, and Strauss, by his "mythical" theory, also endeavored to give them a late origin and a spurious character. But Renan, while sharing their hostility to Christianity as of divine and supernatural character, is constrained by plain evidence to acknowledge the genuineness of Luke, though he holds that all statements implying the supernatural are legendary. Of him Dr. Wace says:†

"No one doubts his perfect familiarity with the whole range of criticism represented by such names as Strauss and Baur, and no one questions his disposition to give full weight to every objection which that criticism can urge. Even without presuming that he is prejudiced on either one side or the other, it will be admitted on all hands that he is more favorably disposed than otherwise to such criticism as we have to meet. When, therefore, with this full knowledge of the literature of the subject, such a writer comes to the

* Preface to Renan's " Vie de Jésus."
† " The Authenticity of the Four Gospels," p. 17.

conclusion that the criticism in question has entirely failed to make good its case on a point like that of the authorship of St. Luke's Gospel, we are at least justified in concluding that critical objections do not possess the weight which unbelievers or skeptics are wont to assign to them. M. Renan, in a word, is no adequate witness to the Gospels, but he is a very significant witness as to the value of modern critical objections to them."

But Renan not only acknowledges that the evidences of Luke's authorship of the Gospel which has his name attached to it and of the Acts of the Apostles are clear, but says he: "To sum up, I admit the four canonical Gospels as serious documents. They all go back to the age which followed the death of Jesus," etc.*

While Renan's theory that the supernatural cannot be admitted led him to reject the Gospels as the divine revelation which we believe them to be, his knowledge of the evidences constrained him to acknowledge that they were "serious documents" and therefore not forgeries, and that they were written at the time when we suppose them to have been written, in "the age which followed the death of Jesus."

When we come to examine the Gospels themselves we find everything to indicate that they

* Preface to " Vie de Jésus," p. lxxxi.

originated at this time and that they were written by the authors whose names they bear. If a book has always borne the name of a writer from its first introduction, and there is no reason to believe that there is any intention to deceive in the matter, we do not hesitate to believe that the person whose name the book bears is its author. If we are asked long afterward to believe that such a person was not the author, but that some one else wrote it, the one making such a demand is under obligation to furnish proof of what he avers.

The Gospels have borne the names of their reputed authors from their first appearance, so far as we can learn. Indeed, everything is in favor of the supposition that the persons whose names they bear are those to whom they have been attributed from the first. We have seen the clear testimony of Irenæus, who could certainly have learned from his teacher, Polycarp, the facts of the case. Polycarp could not have been mistaken, for the last Gospel was written in his lifetime and by his own teacher, according to the statement of Irenæus.

The well-known testimony of Papias of Hierapolis, whom Irenæus calls "a hearer of John and a companion of Polycarp," is clear and explicit as to the authorship of the Gospels of Matthew and Mark.

Eusebius* quotes Papias as saying, " Matthew composed the oracles in the Hebrew tongue, and each one interpreted them as he could."

This shows that the first Gospel was attributed to Matthew from the beginning. The use of the word " oracles," too, reminds one of the expression of Paul in Romans iii. 1, where he evidently means the Holy Scriptures. Papias, it would seem, then, instead of referring only to the discourses of our Lord, intends to rank the Gospel of Matthew with the rest of the Holy Scriptures.

Of Mark Papias says: " Mark, having become the interpreter of Peter, wrote down accurately everything that he remembered. . . . So, then, Mark made no mistake while he thus wrote down some things as he remembered them, for he made it his one care not to omit anything that he heard or to set down any false statement."

Thus we see that these two Gospels bearing the names of Matthew and Mark are attributed to them as their authors by a man who was a younger contemporary of the last of the apostles.

Now, as we turn to examine the contents of those books whose traditionary authorship, from the very age in which they were produced and for a long time after it, was undisputed,† we shall

* " Hist. Eccl.," book iii., chap. xxxix.
† The case of the Alogi no real exception. See Neander's " Hist. of Ch.," p. 374 (Rose's trans.).

find them exhibiting several characteristics which confirm the tradition concerning them and attest their genuineness.

There is one thing about the first three Gospels which stamps them as productions of the period preceding the destruction of Jerusalem in the year 70. In all of them there is recorded that remarkable prophecy of our Saviour about the destruction of Jerusalem, His own coming, and the end of the world.

These events are all evidently in the future when these Gospels are penned. The prophecy, recorded with some variations of language in the different Gospels, has one marked characteristic in each and all of them. That characteristic makes it very difficult to interpret. It is this: the future events are so described that it is not absolutely certain in some expressions which of the events named is referred to. Indeed, some parts of the prophecy seem to be capable of bearing different senses, in one of which it will be applicable to one of these events, while in another it would apply to another of them. Like many other prophecies, it seems to have the " springing and germinant " quality of Bacon's celebrated aphorism, having different fulfilments in various ages and " reaching its height and fullness in some one age."

It is the oak-in-the-acorn principle. Some of the first fulfilments may be as insignificant, when compared to the "height and fullness" which it is to reach, as the mustard-seed compared to the future "tree" in whose branches the birds will build. These great events are in this prophecy foreshortened and apparently intermingled, and this characteristic marks the date of the writing as preceding that first fulfilment, which occurred in the destruction of the Holy City. If it had already occurred the writer could not but have seen that it was a different thing historically from the second advent and the end of the world.

To use a very plain and homely illustration, when we are traveling along a road beside which a telegraph runs, the poles ahead of us may seem very close together, and from certain positions we do not see the spaces between them; but when we pass one of these, we see from our changed point of view that there is a wide interval between it and the next one ahead, against which it just now seemed to be leaning. These writers evidently had not passed the first of the events, and hence the foreshortening and commingling of these great events with much in common in great principles, but widely divided in time.

When we come to examine the fourth Gospel we find that it is written as if by an eye-witness of much that is related, while the author, evidently from delicacy, often studiously refrains from mentioning his own name. This is espe-

cially noticeable in his mention (i. 37) of " the
two disciples " who heard John the Baptist say as
he looked on Jesus, " Behold the Lamb of God!"
" One of the two," he informs us, " was Andrew,
Simon Peter's brother." He does not mention
that he himself was the other, but only leaves it
to be inferred. The author was evidently the
questioner at the table as to who the traitor was,
but he does not mention his name. Instead of
this, he draws the ever-memorable picture in
which those who love the Lord Jesus have ever
since recognized him. " Now there was leaning
on Jesus' bosom one of His disciples, whom Jesus
loved." At the cross, in that tenderest of all the
scenes about it, the author's name does not appear. " When Jesus therefore saw His mother,
and the disciple standing by, whom He loved,"
are his words. At the sepulcher Peter is named,
but he himself is " the other disciple." At the
Sea of Galilee, in the wonderful scene of the miraculous draft of fishes, and the restoration of
Peter by the risen Lord, he is still " the disciple
whom Jesus loved." And in the next to the last
verse of the Gospel we are told, " This is the disciple which testifieth of these things, and wrote
these things: and we know that his testimony is
true." He is still the unnamed eye-witness. But
the veil of delicacy which John uses does not and
was not intended to obscure his authorship of this

Gospel, as this distinct and clear attestation at the close of it shows.*

Thus, while on entering this central apartment with its four portals we saw over the lintels the superscriptions, " The Gospel according to Matthew," "according to Mark," "according to Luke," " according to John," we find, as we come within and examine the handiwork and the material, indications that this structure was builded in " *the age which followed the death of Jesus,*" and by those who were " eye-witnesses of His majesty," or their companions, to whom, with the vividness of personal knowledge, they communicated the wonderful facts and words which form the foundation-stones and unearthly splendors of that monument of divine grace and love for lost men which we call " The New Testament."

There are personal reminiscences like these: " We *beheld* His glory, the glory as of the only begotten of the Father;" " That which was from the beginning, *which we have heard, which we have seen with our eyes, which we have looked upon, and our hands have handled, of the Word of life;* . . . that which *we have seen* and *heard* declare we unto you." It is all in the manner of another eye-witness who says, " For He received from God

---

* The supposition of Godet and others, that these are the words of editors, is plausible; but the style of the last chapter proclaims it John's.

the Father honor and glory, when there came such a voice to Him from the excellent glory, This is My beloved Son, in Whom I am well pleased. And this voice which came from heaven *we heard, when we were with Him in the holy mount*" (2 Pet. i. 17, 18).

The omissions in the fourth Gospel can be explained only by supposing that it was written after the other three and that the author knew their contents. The omission of an account of the selection of the twelve apostles is one of these. Christ's Galilean ministry is omitted, while accounts of five sojourns in Jerusalem and Judea are given. The extended discourses at and after the institution of the Lord's Supper are given, but the Sermon on the Mount and the great body of the parables are omitted. The account of the institution of this sacrament is omitted, while the scene of it is portrayed at length, and many occurrences and sayings omitted by the other evangelists are inserted here. This shows quite plainly that the author of this Gospel knew that the things omitted had been already recorded. This is no doubtful evidence (and the evidence of silence is often the most convincing) of an apostle that the synoptic Gospels were already written when he wrote.

The closer our examination of all these Gospels, and other books of the New Testament, the clearer will be the evidence that they were written in the apostolic age.

The first four epistles, Romans, 1 and 2 Corinthians, and Galatians, are allowed even by the most exacting critics, even by F. Christian Baur himself, to have been written by Paul. We find that the rest which bear his name also bear clear marks of the same hand. No writings ever more unmistakably bore the impress of their author. The claim in the epistles, unvarying tradition, the style, and the "undesigned coincidence" with the Acts of the Apostles, unite in testifying to Paul as their author. But in addition to this, Paul, the unique character that he is, is seen and felt everywhere in them.

Phidias is said to have executed that wonder of art, the shield of Athena, in such a way that portraits of his patron, Pericles, and of himself, the sculptor, also, were seen on it. In all the Pauline epistles the lineaments of Christ shine forth, but everywhere in them we find Paul ever unconsciously revealing himself also, in the act of portraying his Master.

The abrupt conclusion of the Acts of the Apostles indicates that Luke, of whom Paul said, "Only Luke is with me," perished with the apostle. The sudden breaking off without recording Paul's martyrdom is most naturally explained by supposing that the Acts was written before that event.

Without further particularizing as to the evidence of the authorship of the books of the New Testament, it is sufficient to draw attention for a moment to the way in which they fit into the history of the time in which they claim to have been written, to show that they could have been written at no other period.

For one thing, the political peculiarities of the period covered by the transactions related in the New Testament were such that no writer could have forged the accounts at a later time without falling into many mistakes. The government of the country was administered in five distinct forms during this period. Even the astute and clear-headed Tacitus seems to have been unable successfully to thread the mazes of a situation so complicated, and the most skilful forger who in the second century should have attempted the telling of such a story as that of the Gospels and the Acts would have tripped at almost every step. How is it with the New Testament writers? Here is the answer of one who has examined the matter most carefully:

" The writers of the New Testament nowhere betray any perplexity. They mark, quite incidentally and without the slightest trace of strain or effort, the various phases, extraordinary as they were, of the civil government of Palestine. Thus at the era of the advent we (1) find the country

subject to the sole government of Herod the
Great (Matt. ii. 1 ; Luke i. 5) ; then (2) we have
his dominions partitioned among his sons, while
one, Archelaus, reigns over Judea with the title of
king (Matt. ii. 22) ; then (3) we see Judea reduced to
the condition of a Roman province, while Galilee,
Iturea, and Trachonitis continue under native
princes (Luke iii. 1) ; then (4) in the person of
Herod Agrippa I. we have the old kingdom of
Palestine restored (Acts xii. 1) ; and finally (5)
we observe the whole country reduced under
Roman rule, and Roman procurators (Felix, Acts
xxiii. 24; Festus, Acts xxiv. 27) reëstablished,
while a certain degree of deference is paid to
Herod Agrippa II., to whom Festus refers Paul's
case as presenting special difficulties." *

But this is only the vestibule of a great laby-
rinth in which none but persons living in the lands
and in the time of which the books of the New
Testament give us accounts could possibly have
avoided being hopelessly confused.

No attempt will here be made to exhibit in
detail the many complications which would have
furnished snares and pitfalls for any forger who
might have attempted in the second century to
write such accounts. We can only take a passing glance at the situation. The writer just

* " Historical Illustrations of the New Testament Scriptures,"
by Rev. G. F. Maclear, D.D., p. 6.

named has summed up the difficulties which such an attempt would have met under five heads:

1. The political condition of Palestine (just mentioned).
2. Roman emperors and administrators.
3. Jewish kings and princes.
4. Condition of the Jewish nation.
5. The Greek and Roman world.

Under each of these heads there is an intricate array of particulars.

Many with a zeal against Christianity, which sharpened their vision for the discovery of mistakes, have endeavored to show that the writers of the New Testament have in some cases fallen into error, but a fuller investigation and the light of archæological discoveries have shown that their zeal has been " not according to knowledge." A notable case in point is that of the " enrolment " under Augustus, which providentially caused our Lord's mother to go with Joseph to Bethlehem, their " own city," where our Lord was born according to the prophecy which assigned the city of David as the birthplace of the Messiah.

Much has been written to prove that Luke was guilty of an anachronism, because Cyrenius (or Quirinus) became governor of Syria when our Lord was about ten years old.   But, as Maclear says, " There has been no serious refutation of the view, first developed by Zumpt, that Quirinus was *twice* governor, once in B.C. 4, when he began the census, and once in A.D. 6, when he carried it to completion." Suetonius tells of three such enrolments in the reign of Augustus.*

In another case Luke has been accused of making a mistake. He calls Sergius Paulus the "proconsul" ("deputy" in the Authorized Version ") of Cyprus, while many scholars contended that Cyprus was an imperial province and that the title of Sergius Paulus was "propretor." Closer examination, however, has shown that the emperor had transferred Cyprus to the control of the senate, so that the governor's title would properly be "proconsul." Luke's accuracy in the matter has been demonstrated, too, by the discovery of coins of the time, on which is the name of the Emperor Claudius, and the title of the governor as "*proconsul.*" Besides this, an inscription has been discovered bearing the names of two other governors of Cyprus, and in it the title is "proconsul." Thus Luke is thoroughly proved to have been right.

When we see in the New Testament incidental mention of the changing phases of civil administration in Palestine; of the intricate complication of Jewish and Gentile customs; the different modes of marking time; Roman and Jewish watches; civil and ecclesiastical taxes; modes of

* See Maclear, " Historical Illustrations," p. 12.

punishment, Roman and Jewish; the interlacing and intricate adjustments of authority of conquerors and conquered; the Roman emperors of the time; the Roman governors, such as Pilate, Felix, Festus, Sergius Paulus, and Gallio, with glimpses of the characters of all of them and a very full portraiture of some; the Jewish kings and princes, Herod the Great, Archelaus, Herod Antipas, Herod Philip II., Herod Agrippa I., and Herod Agrippa II., and find that they stand before us on these pages with marked characteristics, and then turn to the accounts of Tacitus, Suetonius, and Josephus, and find that the portraitures of these men on their pages are the likenesses of the same persons taken from different points of view, we see a proof, which nothing can overturn, that the men who wrote these books of the New Testament must have lived in " the age which followed the death of Jesus." In the words of the author of " Historical Illustrations ":

" There have been, it must be allowed, signal triumphs won by the genius of poetic and literary imagination; but in all literature there is no other instance of the existence of a number of separate and independent documents bound up in a single volume, relating to an historical period which had its records, its archives, its monuments, and purporting to give an account of events occurring within that period, that can be shown to teem with such minute and truthful incidental allusions to facts, at first sight of the most insignificant import, but which on examination are found to have momentous bearing on those events.

"Every quotation from Josephus, Tacitus, or Suetonius, every fresh archæological exploration in Palestine, Asia Minor, or Greece, only serves to illustrate the minute accuracy with which their titles are given to Roman procurators and proconsuls, Greek 'politarchs,' and Asiatic ediles, and to demonstrate the fidelity with which dual systems of government, of military forces, of capital punishment, of language, and of religious life are described as blending together and coexisting side by side, *at the only period when that coexistence was possible*, among the strangest of all strange people, the Jewish nation, whether living in its own land or scattered throughout the Roman empire."

Here is a jewel of more than earthly price and luster, and here is its setting. Its figure is complicated and absolutely unique, yet its setting exactly fits it. When we apply this story of the gospel to its historical connections and surroundings we find that it fits into them perfectly. As in all literature there is no other such jewel, so in all history there is no other such setting. This story of the Christ belongs to just this place in history, and if the wicked hand of infidelity could tear it away and hide its light the annals of nearly nineteen centuries would be thrown into remediless confusion, while their great series of events would be rendered utterly inexplicable.

We would not only have to erase the brightest pages of the histories of the nations that have marched on to the noblest triumphs and gained the richest rewards of a Christian civilization, but, as the author just quoted has shown, we would have to tear out passages from the annals of heathen writers, like Tacitus, Suetonius, and Pliny the Younger, and make a new edition of the works of Josephus.

The jewel belongs to this setting, the New Testament to this time, the apostolic age.

It is clear that these books of the New Testament were written in the apostolic age. This implies another fact, namely, that they have apostolic authority. For they could not have been universally accepted as authoritative, and have been appealed to by both the orthodox and heretics, unless they had received the approval of those who were recognized as the divinely appointed guides of the church, the apostles of our Lord. Originating in the apostolic age as they did, they would have been instantly repudiated by the apostles and those under their instruction if they had been forgeries. But instead of such repudiation we find indications of their acceptance from the very first. Paul speaks of the Gospel of Luke as " Scripture " on a level with Deuteronomy (I Tim. v. 18): " For the Scripture saith, Thou shalt not muzzle the ox," etc. (Deut. xxv. 4). " And, The laborer is worthy of his hire " (Luke x. 7). Peter speaks of Paul's epistles as wrested by some, like "*the other Scriptures*" (2 Pet. iii. 16).

We have already seen that John's Gospel was evidently supplementary to the three synoptic Gospels, and that the epistles of Paul (and we may say the same of all the epistles and of the Revelation) were built upon the facts of these Gospels as their necessary foundation. Thus in the New Testament books themselves we see plain evidence that some of them were already known when others were written.

But some have asserted that the writers of the New Testament do not themselves claim inspiration and divine authority for their writings. That they do not define the mode of inspiration is freely acknowledged, and there may not be *assertion* of authority anywhere; but is it not *implied* in the whole matter and manner of the New Testament Scriptures? A father may not very frequently remind his children of his position and authority, but the very nature and tone of his commands lead them to feel and recognize his relation to

them as one of authority over them more effec-
tually than any verbal assertion of that authority
could do.

But do not the New Testament writers speak
with a divine authority?

Look at the very opening words of most of the
epistles. We find such expressions as: " Paul, an
apostle (not from men, neither through man, but
through Jesus Christ, and God the Father, who
raised Him from the dead)" (Gal. i. 1, R.V.);
" Paul, an apostle of Jesus Christ by the will of
God " (2 Cor. i. 1 ; Col. i. 1) ; and, " Peter, an apostle
of Jesus Christ " (1 Pet. i. 1) ; " Simon Peter, a ser-
vant and an apostle of Jesus Christ " (2 Pet. i. 1) ; or,
" This then is the MESSAGE which we have heard
of Him, and declare unto you " (1 John i. 5).
Here certainly, not only in tone and manner,
but in plain words, we have authoritative assertions.

Are not the communications in keeping with
such introductions?

In 1 Thessalonians iv. 12 Paul speaks of " the
charge we gave you through the Lord Jesus."
In 2 Thessalonians ii. 15 the authoritative nature
of his preaching and of his letters is plainly asserted : " Hold the traditions which ye were
taught, whether by word, or by epistle of ours."
In 2 Thessalonians iii. 14 the same Christians are
commanded, " If any man obey not our word

by this epistle, note that man, and have no company with him," etc.

The epistles were evidently to be read as Scripture in the assemblies of Christians. In 1 Thessalonians v. 27 the solemn charge is given, " I charge you by the Lord, that this epistle be read unto all the holy brethren."

The Colossians were commanded to read and to circulate these Scriptures, and in the direction given in the body of the epistle (Col. iv. 16) we perhaps have an example of injunctions given through the bearers of other epistles as to the obligation to read and circulate them. The direction is, " And when this epistle is read among you, cause that it be read also in the church of the Laodiceans; and that ye likewise read the epistle from Laodicea." Whether this last-named epistle was our Epistle to the Ephesians, or a duplicate of it sent to Laodicea, or a distinct epistle written to the church of Laodicea and containing matter specially designed for these two churches alone and not intended for the church of future ages, we may never be able to determine. But it evidently comes with the stamp of apostolic authority to the Laodiceans and Colossians.

But what shall we say of the claim of authority when we find at the close of the whole body of writings which we call the New Testament such words as these?

" If any man shall add unto these things, God shall add unto him the plagues that are written in this book : and if any man shall take away from the words of the book of this prophecy, God shall take away his part out of the book of life, and out of the holy city, and from the things which are written in this book."

This book undoubtedly comes with the most solemn assertion of divine authority that we can imagine. As it was evidently intended to stand last among the New Testament writings, is it not evident that, while the primary reference of this warning is to the Book of Revelation, it takes in the whole series of writings of which this book forms the fitting and awful close?

Here some may smile, for it is the fashion to be very free in such matters just now. But reverence and awe, we think, are more fitting as we hear the last words of the Revelation of our Lord, and, longing to be " presented before the presence of His glory with exceeding joy," we cry, " Come, Lord Jesus, come quickly." And " He who testifieth these things saith, Surely I come quickly."

XVIII

THE PORTRAITURE OF CHRIST

225

XVIII

THE PORTRAITURE OF CHRIST

THE crowning proof of the inspiration of the Scriptures is *a quality in them* which the devout reader instinctively recognizes as divine. The precious ointment " bewrayeth itself." This is the evidence on which the faith of the great body of believers rests. They may know nothing of the history of the New Testament and nothing of the many external evidences of the divine origin of Christianity about which scholars reason, but, in common with the much smaller company of the learned, as they bend over this marvel among books they feel that, along with much that is human, there is that which is divine. The characteristics of the many human authors are clearly seen, but a divine Author is recognized as guiding them into all truth. One speaks here as never man spoke. He Himself has said, " My sheep hear My voice," and with the ear of faith they hear it in the words of His gospel. To the

believer the *contents* of the New Testament are its
most convincing evidence.

But even for those who are still among the
spiritually deaf and cannot say when Jesus speaks,
" This is the voice of my Beloved," the New Testament, and especially the Gospels, must bear the
marks of authenticity and inspiration. No theory,
however ingenious, can account for certain features in it if its truthfulness and divine origin be
denied.

Take but one view of the contents of this book :
consider only the *Person* who is revealed in it.
The greatest intellects have recognized in this
wonderful portraiture of Christ in the Gospels a
Person to whom no human hero can be for a
moment compared, and the conclusion of every
capable and unprejudiced student must accord
with the oft-quoted words of Rousseau : " How
petty are the books of the philosophers, with all
their pomp, compared with the Gospels! Can it
be that writings at once so sublime and so simple
are the work of men ? Can He whose life they
tell be Himself no more than a mere man ? Is
there anything in His character of the enthusiast
or ambitious sectary? What sweetness, what
purity in His ways! what touching grace in His
teachings! what loftiness in His maxims! what
profound wisdom in His words! what presence
of mind! what delicacy and aptness in His replies!

what an empire over His passions! Where is the
man, where is the sage who knows how to act, to
suffer, and to die without weakness and without
display?" When we come to study Christ as
portrayed in the Gospels we must conclude, with
Rousseau, that "men do not invent like this!"

That Christ was a real person and not a mere
myth is evident, for one thing, from a most remarkable *unity* in the four descriptions which the
evangelists give of Him.

There are indeed apparent discrepancies between their accounts in some points, such as we
always find in the testimony of independent witnesses about almost any series of occurrences.
These seeming disagreements, while they clearly
prove that the evangelists wrote independently
of one another and thus thoroughly exclude the
theory of collusion as the explanation of this
unity, do not serve in any way to mar it. There
are indeed great differences between the four
accounts.

We find Matthew writing, apparently, chiefly
for "the house of Israel," his "brethren according to the flesh." Consequently, references to
fulfilments of prophecy are prominent, and discourses and parables occupy a large part of his
pages. Christ had long ago said, "I will speak
unto them in parables."

Mark writes succinctly and does not give the

long discourses so fully or so frequently, but pictures vividly the *actions* of Christ, in descriptions which we may easily believe to be the reproduction of the lively impressions on the susceptible mind of Peter, borne in his memory till they were related again and again, with ever fresh interest, to his many hearers, and recorded by Mark, under his direction.*

Luke seems to have viewed Christ chiefly as He who came to seek "*that which was lost*," and he alone gives us the vivid pictures of the lost coin, the lost sheep, and the lost son.

The Gospel of John is almost wholly unlike the others in style and manner and contents. While the first three evangelists write, each evidently without the knowledge of what others had written, John, as we have seen, indicates by omissions and by what he takes for granted as already known that he did know of the other Gospels when he wrote. In this Gospel Christ's *divinity* is the prominent feature, as it is the subject of its very first sentence: "In the beginning was the Word, and the Word was with God, and the Word was God."

There is great diversity, and yet there is wonderful unity, in the portraiture which illumines

---

* See Eusebius, "Hist. Eccl.," book vi., chap. xxv. Hippolytus gives a realistic touch in describing Mark as "he of the maimed finger."

the pages of the four evangelists. The representations of Christ's *treatment of sin and sinners* furnish a striking illustration of this unity in diversity.

Matthew lets us hear the terrible denunciations which He uttered against the " scribes and Pharisees, hypocrites " (Matt. xxiii.), and describes His driving the traders in holy things from the temple. Luke (vii. 36–50) draws the picture of the lost woman kneeling in grief and tearful penitence to hear His assurance of her forgiveness and His approval of her love for Him who had saved her, set in contrast to the cold criticism of Simon, the Pharisee at whose table He was sitting.

It was not because He underrated in any degree the sin of impurity. Matthew lets us hear Him on this point (v. 27–29), and we find that He who was "holy, harmless, and undefiled " had a spirit as sensitive to the slightest taint of impurity as the brightest mirror to the faintest breath, and that He so abhorred and dreaded its effect on His people that He warned against the look that indicated the rise of unholy thought and desire, as adultery in the heart. Yet, while He has nothing but scathing invective for sin in the garb of sanctity, He has nothing but words of tenderness and encouragement for the fallen and penitent.

Here we see apparent diversity in this stern-
ness in the one case and tenderness in the other,
but they exist in harmony in the character of that
Being whose praises the psalmist spoke in the
words (Ps. ci. 1), " I will sing of *mercy* and *judgment*," and of whom the apostle says, " Behold
the *goodness* and *severity* of God."

When Christ is accused of sin by His enemies
it is instructive to see how He answers their al-
legations. One thing appears in all the Gospels:
He never admits that He has sinned in any degree or in any way. For a human being to take
such a position we all feel would be extravagant
folly. We know by observation and experience
what our fallen humanity is, and we know that
the claim by any man of sinlessness would be
presumptuous and false. But Christ never admits
that He has been in fault. His challenge from first
to last is, "Who is he that convicteth Me of sin?"

On one occasion His disciples are charged with
Sabbath-breaking, and He Himself also by impli-
cation, as He was with them and had authority
over them. On the Sabbath morning, when perhaps they had enjoyed no morning meal or had
partaken of an insufficient supply of food, the disciples appeased their hunger by taking advantage
of a law (Deut. xxiii. 25) which allowed them to
pluck with their hands the heads of the wheat
along their way. The Pharisees had no word of

blame for this, for it was lawful; but the disciples rubbed out the grains of wheat in their hands as they went along, and this formed a ground of accusation, as it was the Sabbath, and their critics claimed that this was work and that any work was unlawful on the Sabbath. Our Saviour answers the charge first from the broad principles of common sense, and shows from the case of David that necessity was a valid excuse for this amount of exertion, and that the Sabbath was made for man's benefit and not man for the Sabbath.

But that which should have convinced them that there had been no breach of the Sabbath law by His disciples was the fact that He was " Lord also of the Sabbath day." He was their Lord and the Lord of the Sabbath too, so of course He would not allow them to violate His own ordinance (Matt. xii. 1–8; Mark ii. 23–28; Luke vi. 1–5).

John tells of the charge of Sabbath-breaking made against Him personally on another occasion, because He had on the Sabbath healed the impotent man at the Pool of Bethesda (John v. 1–9). The Jews persecuted Him for doing this good deed, and even sought to slay Him. What is His answer? " But Jesus answered them, My Father worketh hitherto, and I work."

The Father's work of preserving and governing goes on uninterruptedly, and Christ works in unity and unison with the Father. He rises to this sublime truth again, that He is Lord and therefore that His work cannot but be right. Thus on different occasions He is represented by different evangelists as in a contest with these self-righteous ecclesiastics in whose hands the Sabbath law, which was meant to be a source of blessing, had been transformed into an instrument of torture and oppression by their rabbinical additions; and each time He rises to the assertion of His Lordship and divinity.

The Sabbath, designed for man's comfort and relief, a season for the cessation of worldly care and work that the higher nature might have its exercise in spiritual duties and aspirations, an ordinance fruitful in blessing, had in their hands, along with all religion, withered to a dead husk of outward formalities. He who is its Lord asserts His right over it, announces its real design, and thereby rebukes their mistaken censoriousness. He thus answers their accusations practically in the same way in both instances. There is diversity in the occasions, the acts, and the words, but unity in the great principles announced.

Matthew has preserved for us the inspiring words, "Ye are the light of the world." John does not record this saying, but presents us with another which at first sight seems inconsistent with this: "*I* am the Light of the world."

The reconciliation is easy when we find that our Saviour is the light-giver and they are its receivers (John viii. 12), and that He gives light by first giving life (i. 4). " In Him was life; and the life was the light of men." This power of life which He communicates, like the power of electricity under the right condit'ons, breaks out in them into effulgence, and they individually " shine as lights in the world," while together they become " the light of the world." Yet is He the light-giver and therefore "the Light of the world " in the highest sense.

John does not tell of the institution of the Lord's Supper, but he does tell of the mysterious " eating the flesh and drinking the blood of the Son of man," of which spiritual act of receptive faith the Lord's Supper is a visible symbol.

John does not record the parable of the lost sheep, but he does tell of the sheep who can never be lost, and in each case is presented the same loving, all-powerful, divine-human Shepherd, out of whose hand, as out of His Father's, no man or demon can pluck His sheep.

We continually see in the Gospels this emergence of the human and the divine united in Christ. He lies down to sleep so absolutely exhausted that the howling of the winds and the tossing of the billows do not awake Him. He rises up to calm the storm with a word—the word of omnipotence.

He sits weary on the well, hungry and thirsty —a man in His weakness and need. Presently He does what not all the angels of God could do —gives the water of life to human souls, to be in them wells of water springing up into everlasting life; and we see that He is very God, who hath life in Himself even as the Father hath life in Himself.

We find Him at one time taking little children in His arms with human love and tenderness for little ones. At another we behold Him stretching forth, as it were, arms of omnipotence and saying to all humanity, " Come unto ME, all ye that labor and are heavy-laden, and I will give you rest."

We see Him a homeless wanderer, having not where to lay His head, and afterward saying to His disciples, " In My Father's house are many mansions. I go to prepare a place for you."

He hungers and thirsts, and is fed from the loving gifts of devoted followers; yet He invites thousands to partake of feasts that come into being without the labor of a single human hand.

When the Greeks come to Philip, saying, " Sir, we would see Jesus," the announcement to Him leads Him to say strange things. He is about to suffer, and there, under the shadow of the cross, His humanity shrinks and trembles at the near prospect of the untold anguish He is about to endure, and His cry to the Father is like that of Gethsemane, as He prays, " Father, save Me from this hour." Then, in the triumph of submission, with divine knowledge and by divine power He says, " But for this cause came I unto this hour. Father, glorify Thy name." And, as if in spirit hearing in the approach of these Greeks the foot-falls of the countless millions who should in the ages to come crowd to His cross from the heathen world, He exclaims, " And I, if I be lifted up from the earth, will draw all men unto Me."

He speaks with just as perfect ease of the unseen as of the visible, of the eternal as of the temporal. Eternity, past and future, seems as clearly in His view as the present. He walks with easy tread on the sublime summits of truths too high for human discovery and too mysterious for full comprehension when revealed, because His vision was not bounded by mortal horizons, but swept across celestial scenes and took in eternal verities.

He came forth from the Father and therefore could speak of the glory which He had with Him " before the world was "; could speak of Himself while on earth as the " Son of man, which is in heaven "; could say, " He that hath seen Me hath seen the Father," and even, " I and My Father are one."

He is betrayed and arrested, but as He is led

to His trial as a lamb led to the slaughter, by a sentence addressed to one of His followers, He for a moment draws aside the veil that hides the unseen, and we catch a glimpse of an ambush of angelic legions ready at a word to spring to His rescue.

The high priest adjures and threatens Him. His answer presents the august scene in which they who now thirst for His blood and reject and dishonor Him "shall see the Son of man sitting on the right hand of power, and coming in the clouds of heaven."

Here such questions as these suggest themselves:

How is it that these four writers, each in a different way, each giving different facts from the others, or facts seen from a different standpoint, present us a portraiture which is in its great outlines the same in them all, and such a portraiture as has never been conceived by human mind or drawn by human hand before?

Whence comes the inimitable skill by which these four men, each in a somewhat different way, depict a character full of tenderness and ready to bring sympathy, tears, and all possible help to the sufferer, even though that sufferer be a sinner, while this same character is represented as absolutely stern and uncompromising in exposing impenitent iniquity under whatever guise, even that of religion, and pronouncing judgment and doom upon it?

How is it that they all so make this portraiture that we see in each presentation of it the insoluble mystery of the union of a divine and a human nature in one Person?

The only rational answer is that such a Person really existed and that the writers were divinely guided in presenting the portraiture of Him which we have in the Gospels. Men do not invent thus and do not describe thus. Effects necessarily imply causes, and adequate causes. That from the pages of all the evangelists, with all their differences, there should shine forth this unique, marvelous, and infinitely lovely and lovable character, and in them all the *same* character, involves a miracle no less wonderful than the greatest deed of divine power recorded in the Gospels. Says Principal Cairns, in his essay on " Christ, the Central Evidence of Christianity ":

" One Gospel is a marvel; what shall we say of four, each with its distinct plan, its enlargements and omissions, its variations even where most coincident, its problems as yet unsolved, but always yielding something to fresh inquiry, and only making more manifest the unchallengeable oneness and divinity of the history? The difficulties of the Gospels from divergence are as nothing as compared with the impression made by them all of one transcendent creation, and, for my part, if I rejected inspiration I should have reason to be still more astonished. Some slight mistake could so sadly have impaired perfection, or yet more easily lowered divinity; some careless handling might have deranged the balance at the most critical point, or pulled down the structure in hopeless disaster. Yet, though we see how different the plan of each Gospel is, there is not any such trace of failure. The long discourses are left out by Mark, but in action his Christ equals that of Matthew. Luke has his own type both of parable and miracle, but the same inimitable figure starts up from all. The sorest trial to the familiar features comes from the fourth Gospel, without a parable and hardly a miracle like the foregoing, and with so great a flood of novelty, especially toward the end. But unity in diversity is only the more marvelous. The Christ of the fourth Gospel is the Word of God, but He is still the Son of man."

Many have professed to believe that apocryphal "Gospels" and other writings with the claim of apostolic authorship or authorization have as good a right to our confidence as those books which form what we now call the New Testament. This subject cannot be treated with any fullness here, but a mere glance at these documents is sufficient to convince us of the falsity of this claim.

The *late origin* of these spurious " Gospels,"
" Acts," "Epistles," etc., is a proof of the falsity
of the claims which they make or which are made
for them as contemporary and inspired writings.
The fact that our saint's teacher, Irenæus, born
about twenty years after John's death and taught
by Polycarp, who was John's pupil and his contemporary for nearly forty years, represents that
there were only four Gospels, and even endeavors
to show that there *could* be no more, should be
sufficient to convince us of the falsity of such
assertions as have been referred to. But more
absolutely convincing still is the character of the
writings themselves when brought into comparison with the New Testament; and there is no
point in which that comparison brings out a
sharper contrast than that presented in the various
portraitures of Christ in these writings and that
one found in our Gospels.

The following is the testimony of one who has
made a special study of the apocryphal Gospels:

" The case stands thus. Our Gospels present
us with the picture of a glorious Christ; the
mythic Gospels with that of a contemptible one.
Our Gospels have invested Him with the highest
conceivable form of human greatness; the mythic
ones have not ascribed to Him a single action that
is elevated. In our Gospels He exhibits a superhuman wisdom; in the mythic ones a nearly equal

superhuman absurdity.* In our Gospels He is arrayed in all the beauty of holiness; in the mythic ones this aspect is entirely wanting. . . . The miracles of the one and the other are contrasted in every point. A similar opposition of character runs through the whole current of their thought, feeling, morality, and religion."†

The same author tells us of these writings:

"To two of them is assigned as early a date as the end of the first half of the second century; the remainder are of a later date. They enable us to know for certain what was the class of actions which during these times writers of fiction were in the habit of ascribing to our Lord. The incidents which they record are confined to two periods of His life, viz., His childhood and early boyhood, on which our Gospels are almost silent, and His passion and resurrection; and they omit the history of His ministry and teaching. The miracles which they attribute to Him are for the most part of a grotesque character and are devoid of moral impress. They are too painful for quotation, being little better than caricatures of the Holy One of God."‡

* See the account of the resurrection in the so-called Gospel of Peter, for instance; also B. H. Cowper on apocryphal Gospels.
† "The Jesus of the Evangelists," by Prebendary Row, p. 381.
‡ Essay on "The Unity of the Character of the Christ of the Gospels," in "Living Papers," vol. iv.
The most grateful acknowledgments of obligations are due to

Yet it must be remembered that the writers of these spurious productions had the four Gospels before them, and therefore, one would think, would have been able to avoid these absurdities.

Here we may make a passing reference to the way in which fiction has dealt with Christ in our own day. Two instances will suffice to show that where an attempt is made to improve upon the Christ of the Gospels the result is a complete failure.

Sir Edwin Arnold, of " The Light of Asia " fame, has dipped his brush in some very startling colors and produced a picture which no doubt he considers very superior to that of Matthew, Mark, Luke, and John. Yet, with all the advantage of " great eyes, blue and radiant," and though "wine-color shone His hair, glittering and waved," we hardly think that this Christ would have awakened the enthusiasm of a Paul or have moved thousands to face death rather than deny Him.

The same doubt may be expressed about the creation of a still more imaginative writer, Marie Corelli, who in her recent book, " Barabbas," has given her conception of the Saviour. As we look

the essays of Dr. Wace, Canon Row, Godet, Principal Cairns, and Dr. Maclear, published in the very valuable ten volumes called " Living Papers," for whatever of worth is to be found in the last two chapters of this volume.

at her picture, we are glad to say, " This is not
our Lord." That man whom she portrays as
standing at Pilate's bar, " with a slight, dreamy
smile of the beautiful curved lips, and a patient
expression in the down-dropped eyelids," is not
the Christ of the Gospels, the Lord of glory. He
is no weakling, however, for, " still as a statue of
sunlit marble, He stood erect and calm, His white
garments flowing backward from His shoulders
in even, picturesque folds," with arms " suggest-
ing such mighty muscular force as would have
befitted a Hercules."

Such raving, painful to read because it verges
so closely on blasphemy, would not be quoted
but to draw attention to the divinely given self-
restraint of the Gospels, in which the personal
appearance of Christ is *never once mentioned.*

How is it that these " ignorant and unlearned
men," who witnessed the wonderful deeds and
heard the wonderful words of Christ, are never
betrayed into one false touch of an unwise enthusiasm, but have left for us the perfect picture
of Him who has evoked the admiration and
adoration of men for more than eighteen centuries?

Even the great Milton is thought by some to
have drawn on his glowing canvas not the Christ
of the Gospels, but the Christ of Arianism.

Even when the glorious character is taken up

by the hands of genius a false image is the result.
It is besmirched and falsified and belittled in the
very attempt to magnify it. Even in adding false
paint and gilding there is always some awkward-
ness, and it falls from the unskilful hands and is
broken to shivers, so that all who know and love
Christ exclaim, like Mary at the empty tomb,
" They have taken away my Lord!"

How is it that these four men have presented
the one glorious Lord and Saviour without a single
touch of false coloring? How is it that, as this
Christ of the Gospels becomes known, instinctively
the knees bow and the tongues confess " that He
is Lord, to the glory of God the Father "?

The only reasonable explanation is that the
authors of this fourfold description spoke of a real
person who was " the Christ, the Son of the living
God," and were guided in their delineation by
the Holy Spirit, who taught them all things and
brought all things to their remembrance.

As we look from the Gospels into the Acts, the
Epistles, and the Revelation, we find the same
blessed Saviour presented in all. There is no
disappointing change. We find the same Christ
more fully revealed in His relations to us and in
His fitness for the work of our salvation.

In these books we see more clearly than in the
Gospels why He is called " the Christ "—" the
Anointed One." We find that He has been

anointed, not with the oil of consecration, which was applied to mere human prophets, priests, and kings, but with the Holy Ghost without measure. We see why it is that, along with His humanity, *His divinity* is so clearly revealed in all the Gospels and in the other New Testament Scriptures.

We need a Prophet who with a human heart can be touched with the feeling of our infirmities, and with a human tongue can teach us that which He knows with a divine and infallible knowledge. The human soul longs and the human hand feels for the clasp of a hand that can guide infallibly through the darkness of this world up into the glory of that which is to come. Our consciences cry for cleansing in blood that cleanseth from all sin, because it is the blood of a *Man* who is the *only begotten Son of God*. We, together with all that can affect us, have need of the controlling hand of a divine-human King who shall reign "till His enemies [and ours] be made His footstool," and who can bring it about that, in the almost infinite intricacies of the machinery of providence, all things shall work together for our good. We feel the need of a Saviour who can not only present us a perfect *ideal*, the goal to which we are to press forward, but who can, out of His divine fullness, give "grace for grace," and thus enable us to reach that to which we are led to aspire, so that at the last we may "be like Him."

The blessed Saviour, the Christ of the New
Testament, meets all these requirements of our
case, and as soon as the penitent soul comes to
know Him the recognition is a joyful one. The
song which breaks from the lips is:

> "Thou, O Christ, art all I want,
> All in all in Thee I find."

We may search all history and all literature, but
we shall find no other like Him. More than this,
we might take all the noblest characters presented
by enthusiastic admirers, who have skilfully drawn
a veil over their faults while they have extolled
their virtues, and we might cull the choicest at-
tributes from all these, and unite them to make
one character which should combine in itself the
excellences of all, and yet we should not have a
CHRIST. Should we go to the realms of fancy,
to fiction, to poetry, to the drama, yea, even to
mythology, with its divinities and impossible
heroes, yet we could not from them all make up
a CHRIST. Still He would be to this as Hyperion
to a satyr.

When all human genius, in all ages and all
lands, has never invented such a character, can
we suppose each of these four "ignorant and unlearned men" capable of doing it, and each in a
somewhat different way from the other three?

To ask the question is to answer it. Thus,

following the rays of our saint's search-light, we have found, standing in the first century, the completed temple of revelation.

As we have looked from room to room, from the great central shrine of the Gospels to the chambers of the Acts and the Epistles, and down the long vista of the corridor of The Revelation, we have seen mirrored in each, with some differences of light or shade or point of view, *the same Christ Jesus*, the divine-human Redeemer and blessed Saviour. Mind and heart join in saying, This is "He whom my soul loveth." This is One in whom is "life; and the life is the light of men." From this temple, completed in the first century, the light has shone out through all the centuries that have followed.

Guilty Rome placed herself between this light and the people, as the moon comes between the sun and the earth to produce an eclipse, and the long, cruel Dark Ages—that "break of a thousand years in the history of civilization"—came; and now, wherever she can shut out the light from the people, the shadows still linger. But wherever the Bible has gone and been received, there blessings immeasurable have followed. This radiance has awakened the human intellect and led it to its most brilliant exploits. It has guided in the path of all true progress. It has lighted the lamps of learning, and colleges and universities have sprung up and flourished in its beams. Good government, abundant charities, happy homes, glorious characters, and saved souls have been its fruits. Can this be a false light?

Ezekiel in his vision saw waters flowing from the sanctuary, and was told: " Everything shall LIVE whither the river cometh. . . . And by the river upon the bank thereof, on this side and on that side, shall grow all trees for meat, whose leaf shall not fade, neither shall the fruit thereof be consumed: it shall bring forth new fruit according to his months, because their waters they issued out of the sanctuary : and the fruit thereof shall be for meat, and the leaf thereof for medicine."

Thus He who is the *Light* sends forth from the fountain of the temple of revelation that stream which gives *life* wherever it flows. At its coming to any people who receive it, the wilderness and the solitary place are glad for them, and the desert rejoices and blossoms as the rose.

This Book has done more to benefit and bless mankind than all other books together. Can it be false, then? If so, the most poisonous fountain sends forth the purest and most healthful stream, and we can gather grapes of thorns and figs of thistles, and the corrupt tree brings forth good fruit. In other words, TO SUPPOSE THE NEW TESTAMENT A SPURIOUS AND FALSE BOOK

INVOLVES THE SUPPOSITION THAT THE INDIS-SOLUBLE TIE BETWEEN CAUSE AND EFFECT IS BROKEN—an unspeakable absurdity.

He is the "true Light" who has brought blessings ineffable to all hearts and homes, to all tribes and nations, that have received Him. The only rational conclusion is that the Holy Scriptures, the Bible in the Old and New Testaments, thus revealing Him to the world, must be the Word of God.

Looking over the sad world that so sorely needs Him, we would say:

> " Waft, waft, ye winds, His story,
>   And you, ye waters, roll,
> Till, like a sea of glory,
>   It spreads from pole to pole."

www.ingramcontent.com/pod-product-compliance
Lightning Source LLC
Chambersburg PA
CBHW030401270326
41926CB00009B/1207